SHARES
& TAXATION

SHARES
& TAXATION

A Practical Guide to Saving Tax on Your Shares

Jimmy B. Prince

Wrightbooks

First published 2010 by Wrightbooks
an imprint of John Wiley & Sons Australia, Ltd
42 McDougall Street, Milton Qld 4064

Office also in Melbourne

Typeset in Adobe Garamond 12.5/15.5pt

National Library of Australia Cataloguing-in-Publication data:

Author:	Prince, Jimmy B.
Title:	Shares and taxation: a practical guide to saving tax on your shares / Jimmy B Prince.
ISBN:	9781742469560 (pbk.)
Notes:	Includes index.
Subjects:	Investments—Taxation—Australia.
	Dividends—Taxation—Australia.
	Capital gains tax—Australia.
	Value-added tax—Australia.
	Stockholders—Australia.
	Corporations—Investor relations—Australia.
Dewey Number:	332.6042

Cover image ($100 note) © iStockphoto.com/robynmac

Printed in Australia by McPherson's Printing Group

10 9 8 7 6 5 4 3 2 1

Disclaimer
The material in this publication is of the nature of general comment only, and does not represent professional advice. It is not intended to provide specific guidance for particular circumstances and it should not be relied on as the basis for any decision to take action or not take action on any matter which it covers. Readers should obtain professional advice where appropriate, before making any such decision. To the maximum extent permitted by law, the author and publisher disclaim all responsibility and liability to any person, arising directly or indirectly from any person taking or not taking action based upon the information in this publication.

Contents

About the author

Jim Prince is a fellow of CPA Australia and a tax specialist. He is a former lecturer and tutor in income tax law at LaTrobe University, and teaches a number of wealth creation courses for the CAE in Melbourne. He has authored several investment books including *Tax for Australians For Dummies* and *Building Wealth & Loving It*, and has written articles for *Your Mortgage* magazine and <http://thebull.com.au>. In 2000 Jim was nominated for an Adult Learners Week 2000 outstanding tutor award.

In his earlier years Jim worked for the Australian Taxation Office and also consulted to CPA Australia 'Technicall'.

Preface

When you invest in the sharemarket you will be relying on major public companies listed on the Australian Securities Exchange (ASX) running profitable businesses for steady income and capital growth. Unfortunately, when you receive a dividend or make a capital gain on sale of your shares, you're legally obligated to share the spoils of your good fortune with the Australian Taxation Office (ATO).

The tax issues associated with owning shares can at times be mind-boggling and difficult to understand. There are specific tax laws in respect of how dividends and franking credits are taxed, what you can and can't claim as a tax deduction, and how to calculate a capital gain or capital loss. There are also numerous taxation rulings you'll need to comply with the moment you start buying shares. To complicate matters further you'll need to establish at the outset whether you're carrying on a business as a share trader or you're a share investor, as different tax rules apply to share traders and share investors. Unfortunately, when it comes to tax you simply can't guess whether you're one or the other, and if you get it wrong the Tax Office could impose stiff penalties. The good news is you can always go to a registered tax agent if you get into difficulty. But don't give up all hope just yet!

The purpose of writing this book is to give you the basic skills (and confidence) for dealing with the taxation of shares. The book explains in simple terms core tax principles with numerous tax tips, potential tax traps and practical case studies to reinforce the learning process. Emphasis is placed on the following core tax principles:

- how share traders and share investors are taxed

- owning shares in different legal structures

- dividends and franking credits

- what expenses are tax deductible

- how to calculate a capital gain and capital loss

- borrowing to buy shares

- taxation of derivatives

- record-keeping and tax audits.

Throughout the book you'll find at your fingertips numerous references to taxation publications, tax rulings and tax determinations that the tax professionals use to solve specific problems. You can quickly find these publications and tax rulings on the ATO website. The book also provides a historic timeline of major events in shares and taxation. So why pay someone $250 an hour to solve a problem when you can read this book and find the answer yourself? This practical guide can continue to be used to help you find a particular publication or tax ruling you may wish to consult from time to time.

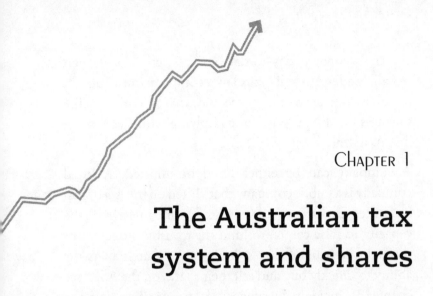

Chapter 1

The Australian tax system and shares

If you want to make money investing in shares it's essential that you have a general understanding of how the sharemarket operates and how your share transactions are taxed. In this chapter I cover the basics and guide you through the key taxation issues associated with investing in shares.

Investing in shares: back to basics

Under Australian corporations law a company is a separate legal entity. This means it has an independent existence and can carry on a business in its own name. Shareholders appoint company directors to manage and run the company's day-to-day business activities on their behalf. Under Australian tax law a company must appoint a public officer within three months of commencing business for the purposes of complying with the Income Tax Assessment Act.

A company can be either listed or unlisted. A listed company is a public company that's listed on the Australian Securities Exchange (ASX). Listed companies have the capacity to raise capital to fund their business operations through the issue of shares. It also gives shareholders the ability to quickly buy and sell their shares on the ASX (see chapter 3). Incidentally, when a company is floated on the ASX, you can buy the shares direct from the company. This is referred to as buying shares in the primary market. You'll need to read the company's prospectus and complete an offer application form to get these shares. Once the company is listed you can only buy shares in the secondary market (namely, on the ASX). In contrast, an unlisted company is one that's not listed on the ASX, which means you may not be given the opportunity to invest in these companies.

The All Ordinaries index (comprising the top 500 companies listed on the ASX) and the S&P/ASX 200 index are the two key indices Australia uses to measure the market direction of companies listed on the ASX. The S&P/ASX 200 index (comprising more than 90 per cent of total market capitalisation) is also a major investment benchmark index that's used to measure the performance of Australia's leading managed funds such as share trusts (see chapter 4).

When you buy shares listed on the ASX you'll become a shareholder (or part owner) of a major public company (such as BHP Billiton or CBA). After you buy your shares the company will issue a 'holding statement' setting out the number of shares you bought (see chapter 3). The shares you will normally buy and sell are ordinary shares. Ordinary shares give shareholders certain rights, such as:

- receiving a copy of the company's annual report and a vote at the annual general meeting

- receiving a distribution of company profits, referred to as dividends, plus franking credits if the dividends are franked. Under Australian tax law you will need to include both the dividend and franking credit as part of your assessable income, and you can claim a franking credit tax offset (see chapter 5)

- receiving a return of capital to shareholders. Under Australian tax law you will need to adjust the cost base and reduced cost base of the shares you own for capital gains tax (CGT) purposes. If the return of capital is more than the cost base the difference is treated as a capital gain (see chapter 6). Incidentally, the Tax Office has ruled moneys paid by a company to its shareholders as a capital return do not ordinarily constitute a dividend (see chapter 5)

- the ability to purchase additional shares direct from the company by participating in the company's 'dividend reinvestment plan' and 'rights issues'. These shares are normally issued to shareholders at a discount and no brokerage or GST is payable (see chapter 5).

Tax tip

Under Australian tax law companies are classified as either 'public companies' (for instance, companies listed on the ASX) or 'private companies'. Private companies are subject to special tax rules with respect to issues such as advances and loans to shareholders and access to losses incurred in earlier years. See chapter 4 for more details.

How the Australian tax system works

Under Australian tax law, tax is levied on your taxable income. The Australian taxation system uses the following formula to calculate taxable income.

Total assessable income – allowable deductions = taxable income.

At the end of the financial year—which commences on 1 July and ends on 30 June—Australian residents are required to disclose the taxable income they have derived from all sources, whether in or out of Australia. This means if you receive a foreign dividend you'll need to disclose the amount in your individual tax return (for more details see chapter 5). On the other hand, if you're a non-resident of Australia, you're only required to disclose taxable income that has an Australian source (for more details see appendix B).

For individuals, tax is levied on your taxable income on a progressive basis. This means the more income you earn the more tax you're liable to pay. The amount of tax payable depends on your marginal rates of tax (which can vary between 0 per cent and 45 per cent). If you are an Australian resident the tax payable is reduced by any domestic tax offsets or credits you may be entitled to claim (for instance, dividend franking credits). Incidentally, if you derive a foreign dividend and tax was withheld from the payment you can claim a foreign tax credit (see chapter 5). You may also be liable to pay a Medicare levy if your taxable income is above a statutory amount. The Medicare levy is 1.5 per cent of your taxable income. On the other hand, a company pays a flat 30 per cent rate of tax on the taxable income it derives and no Medicare levy will apply. (At the time of writing, the Federal Labor Government has proposed to reduce the company tax rate to 29 per cent in the 2013–14 financial year and to 28 per cent in the 2014–15 financial year.)

At a glance: how you're taxed

This is how the Australian tax system works:

- Resident individuals pay tax on a progressive basis at their marginal rates of tax; the first $6000 you earn is tax-free.

- Capital gains are liable to tax at your marginal rates of tax, but you can claim a 50 per cent CGT discount if you hold CGT assets (for instance, shares) for more than 12 months.

- Australian residents are liable to pay a 1.5 per cent Medicare levy.

- Australian residents can claim certain tax offsets (for instance, dividend franking credits and a low income tax offset).

- Companies pay a flat 30 per cent rate of tax on the entire amount of taxable income they derive (see chapter 4).

- A partnership is not liable to pay tax; all income and losses must be distributed to the individual partners (see chapter 4).

- A trust does not pay tax; all income is assessed to either the trustee or beneficiaries (see chapter 4).

- Complying superannuation funds pay a flat 15 per cent rate of tax; but the rate is 45 per cent if the fund is a non-complying superannuation fund (see chapter 4).

 Tax tip

If you want to find out your current marginal rate of tax you can visit the ATO website <www.ato.gov. au>; go to 'Find a rate or calculator' then 'Individual income tax rates'.

Coming to terms with self-assessment

Australia's tax system operates on a self-assessment basis. Under self-assessment, when you lodge your annual tax return for individuals the Australian Taxation Office

(ATO) will ordinarily accept its contents as being true and correct. Apart from correcting any noticeable errors or omissions no further action is taken. Shortly after you lodge your tax return the Tax Office will issue a notice of assessment setting out such details as:

- the assessment notice sequence number

- the date of issue

- your name and address

- your taxable income

- the tax payable on your taxable income

- the Medicare levy amount

- pay-as-you-go (PAYG) withholding credits (for instance, tax withheld from unfranked dividends; see chapter 2)

- credit for any PAYG instalments raised

- tax offsets and other credits (for instance, dividend franking credits)

- the actual amount payable/refundable

- the due date for payment of tax.

Under self-assessment the ATO reserves the right to audit your tax affairs to check whether you're complying with the Income Tax Assessment Act. For instance, the Tax Office will regularly compare the dividends you must disclose in your tax return with the records of the paying companies. This is to check whether you had disclosed the correct amount. So you'll need to keep proper records and receipts to verify and substantiate what you had disclosed in your tax return (see chapter 9). Under this system you can apply for a private ruling regarding any tax matters you are not sure of (for instance, whether you're carrying on a business as a share trader). The Tax Office will examine your request and give you a written response as to how it would interpret the law in respect of the issue you had raised. There is no fee for this service.

 Tax tip

The Australian Taxation Office is the federal government authority responsible for administering the Income Tax Assessment Act. As you will find throughout this book the ATO regularly issues Tax Office publications, income tax rulings, tax determinations and interpretative decisions to explain specific tax issues that need to be clarified and brought to your attention. These publications are free of charge, and are issued to help you to comply with Australia's complex tax laws. You can download these publications and rulings from the ATO website <www.ato.gov.au>.

Getting professional help

If you're experiencing difficulty preparing your individual tax return or you're not sure what to do, you can contact your local Tax Office and/or visit a recognised tax adviser (such as a registered tax agent). A tax agent is a person who is authorised to give you advice in respect of managing your tax affairs, and can prepare and lodge a tax return on your behalf. In return you will be charged a fee for their services, which incidentally is a tax deductible expense. A tax agent can also attend an ATO audit and can lodge an objection if you're dissatisfied with your notice of assessment.

 Tax trap

If you do not lodge your individual tax return by 31 October you could be liable to pay a late lodgement penalty. You can avoid this penalty if you visit a tax agent. This is because tax agents are given a general extension of time to lodge income tax returns on behalf of their clients.

 Tax tip

There are two ways you can lodge your tax return. You can fill out a paper tax form included in Tax Pack for individuals and post it to your local Tax Office, or you can lodge your tax return online using e-tax. You can get a copy of Tax Pack for individuals from your local newsagent or you can contact your local ATO.

At a glance: shares and tax

Under Australian tax law the way your share transactions are taxed is primarily dependent on whether you are carrying on a business as a share trader or you are a share investor. This is because different tax rules apply to share traders and share investors. There are a number of tests to check whether you are one or the other. I discuss this matter in much detail in chapter 2.

Checklist

The following checklist provides a quick overview of the key taxation issues associated with owning shares. These issues will be discussed in greater detail in later chapters.

Dividend payments

Companies normally declare and pay two dividends to their shareholders each year. They are an interim or mid-year dividend and a final or end-of-year dividend. Under Australian tax law, dividends are liable to tax when they are paid or credited to your account (see chapter 5).

Dividend franking credits

Australia has adopted a dividend imputation system in respect to the payment of dividends. Under this system, when a company declares a dividend it must state whether the dividend is franked or unfranked. Franked means the company had paid tax on the profits it derived, and this can be passed on to resident shareholders in the form of a franking credit or tax offset. But if the dividend is unfranked you won't receive a franking credit (see chapter 5). Shareholders will need to include both the dividend and franking credit as part of their assessable income. They will be taxed on the grossed-up amount and can claim a franking credit tax offset. Incidentally, the Tax Office will refund any excess franking credits to you.

Trading profits and losses

If you carry on a share trading business your profits and losses will be taxed in the same way as a person who carries on a business as a plumber, motor mechanic or accountant. This means your sales are assessable income, your purchases are a tax deductible expense, and shares not yet sold are treated as trading stock on hand. But if you are a share investor your profits and losses will be assessable under the CGT provisions (see chapter 2).

Unrealised capital gains

Under Australian tax law, unrealised capital gains are ordinarily not liable to tax. This means it's possible for you to hold shares in companies that are continually increasing in value, and no tax is payable until there is a disposal. A disposal (CGT event) will ordinarily arise when there is a change in ownership. For instance, a disposal will ordinarily arise when you sell your shares or give them away as a gift to your partner or children. Under the CGT provisions, if you own shares for more than 12 months only half the capital gain is liable to tax at your marginal rates of tax. The balance is exempt and excluded from your assessable income. But if you sell your shares within 12 months of buying them the entire capital gain is liable to tax at your marginal rates of tax. For more details see chapter 6.

 Tax tip

A company may offer its shareholders a discount on certain products or services it sells to the general public. The fringe benefit you stand to gain will enhance the overall return on your investment. Under Australian tax law this fringe benefit is not liable to income tax.

Interest on borrowings

Interest on money borrowed to buy shares for the purposes of deriving assessable income is ordinarily a tax deductible expense. Under Australian tax law, if your interest payments exceed your dividend payments, the net loss can be deducted from any other assessable income you derive (for instance, your salary and wages, business profits and investment income). This is referred to as negative gearing. For more details see chapter 7.

Allowable deductions

Under Australian tax law, expenditure that you incur in deriving assessable income (such as dividends) or that is incurred in carrying on a business (for instance, you're a share trader) for the purposes of deriving assessable income (such as share trading profits) is a tax deductible expense. For more details see chapters 2 and 5.

Offsetting a capital loss

Under Australian tax law an unrealised capital loss cannot be used until there is a disposal (for instance, you sell your shares). If you make a capital loss on sale, the capital loss can only be offset against a capital gain you make on sale of other shares (or CGT assets) that you own. If you make no capital gains in the financial year you incur a capital loss, the capital loss can be carried forward for an indefinite period, and can be offset against any future capital gains you make. When a capital loss is offset against a capital gain you will effectively save paying tax on the capital gain you made. The tax you save will indirectly reduce the amount of the capital loss you incurred (see chapter 5).

 Tax trap

Keep in mind you can only claim a 50 per cent CGT discount *after* you deduct all your current and prior year capital losses. For more details see chapter 6.

Useful references

- Australian Securities Exchange website <www.asx. com.au>—go to 'Education and resources', then click on 'Education', then see 'What are shares', 'Getting started in shares' and 'Dividends explained'.

- Australian Securities & Investments Commission <www.fido.asic.gov.au>—go to 'About financial products' and click on 'Shares'.

- *Tax for Australians For Dummies* (John Wiley & Sons Australia Ltd).

Australian Taxation Office publications

- *Do you own shares?*

- *Income from dividends*

- *Investment essentials*

- *Personal investor's guide to capital gains tax* (NAT 4152)

- *Private rulings and advice essentials*

- *Self-assessment and the taxpayer*

- *Shares—helping you to avoid common mistakes* (NAT 73418)

- *Tax Pack for individuals*

- *Tax Pack Supplement for individuals with investments*

- *Tax-smart investing: what share investors need to know* (NAT 14125)

- *You and your shares* (NAT 2632)

- *Your notice of assessment*

Chapter 2

Share trader or share investor: why all the fuss?

Although you may be considered a share trader under commercial law (for instance, you register your business name), or you may think you're a share trader, for the purposes of the Income Tax Assessment Act you may find this is not the case. There are stringent tests you'll need to satisfy before you can call yourself a share trader for tax purposes. The reason the Australian Taxation Office (ATO) is so pedantic is because different tax rules apply to share traders and share investors. So you'll need to get it right at the outset. In this chapter I identify and explain the taxation issues associated with being a share trader and a share investor.

Defining who you are

With respect to share transactions, the way you calculate your taxable income is primarily dependent on whether the ATO classifies you as carrying on a share trading business or treats your activities as similar to that of a share investor. When tax is involved it's a black-and-white issue as to whether you're one or the other. And this of course comes down to a question of fact. Whenever the terms 'share trader' and 'share investor' are used throughout this book it implies the following.

Share trader

You are carrying on a business trading in shares (and/or derivatives) if the predominant purpose is making a profit (and your shares are said to be held on 'revenue account'). If this is the case:

- Proceeds from the sale of your shares will be treated as assessable income; the income is ordinarily recognised when you receive the payment.

- The dividends you receive are treated as assessable income.

- The shares you purchase are treated as trading stock and are a tax deductible expense.

- At the end of each financial year you will need to bring to account your stock on hand (namely shares not yet sold).

- You can claim certain tax deductions commonly associated with carrying on a business; for instance, your contributions to a complying superannuation fund may qualify as a tax deductible expense.

Share investor

You are a share investor if the predominant purpose for buying your shares is to derive dividends (and your shares are said to be held on 'capital account'). If this is the case:

- Your share purchases are capital in nature and not a tax deductible expense.

- The dividends you receive are treated as assessable income.

- You can only claim a tax deduction if the purpose of the outgoing is to derive dividends (see chapter 5).

- The profits and losses you make on sale of your shares will fall for consideration under the capital gains tax (CGT) provisions. This means they will be classified as capital gains and capital losses and you will be taxed as follows:

  - If you sell shares you purchased within 12 months, the entire capital gain is liable to tax.

  - If you sell shares you've held for more than 12 months, only 50 per cent of the capital gain is liable to tax.

- If you make a capital loss you cannot deduct it from other assessable income you derive (for instance, salary and wages, business profits and investment income like dividends).

- You can only offset a capital loss from a capital gain.

- If you make no capital gains in the financial year you make a capital loss, the capital loss is quarantined and can be offset against any capital gains you may make in the future.

 Tax tip

The ATO has issued a publication *Carrying on a business of share trading* to explain the difference between a share trader and a share investor. You can contact your local Tax Office or you can download a copy from its website <www.ato.gov.au>.

Carrying on a share trading business: the tests you had to have

The Income Tax Assessment Act defines a 'business' for tax purposes as 'any profession, trade, employment, vocation or calling, but does not include occupation as an employee'. Whether you're carrying on a share trading business is a question of fact. The Tax Office uses the following key tests to determine how your gains and losses are taxed.

- *Your intention to make a profit.* Your share transactions must be entered into for the purposes of making a profit. Share traders are not overly concerned or preoccupied with deriving dividends (as is normally the case if you are a share investor).

- *Whether you are operating in a businesslike manner.* This test checks whether your transactions have a commercial flavour; for instance:

  - you have a business plan

  - you have access to immediate funds

  - you conduct your own research (for instance, daily analysis of share price trends) and/or you regularly consult a stockbroker

  - you keep proper records of your share trading activities

  - you have an account with a stockbroker

  - you maintain a computer and internet access, trade online and use computer trading software programs to help you make an informed decision when to buy or sell

  - you keep up to date with current developments, seek professional advice, attend training courses and read share magazines and the financial newspapers

  - you are aware of fundamental analysis and/or technical analysis, and you apply their respective principles when making a decision when to buy or sell (for more details see glossary).

- *Your regular trading patterns.* There is some organisation and commercial behaviour in your decision-making patterns. For instance, you regularly buy in the morning and sell in the afternoon; you're reluctant to hold shares over the weekend; you're eager to sell if your shares increase in value by a predetermined amount (for instance, 10 per cent).

- *The frequency of trades you do each year.* For instance, you do 400 trades each year. As a rule of thumb the more trades you do the greater the chance the Tax Office will classify you as a share trader for the purposes of the Tax Act.

- *The amount of capital you have invested.* The ATO has ruled that capital is not considered a major test in determining whether you're carrying on a share trading business. But you'll need to have a sufficient sum on hand to bankroll your ongoing share transactions (especially if you incur substantial losses).

- *Whether you are operating to a set plan, budget or target.* For instance, you have:

  □ set aside a certain amount of capital to bankroll your share trades

  □ a plan to make a certain amount of profit from each trade you enter into

  □ stop-loss strategies to limit potential losses you may incur

  □ specific plans/strategies in place as to when you should enter and exit the sharemarket.

- *Whether you are maintaining proper records.* For instance, you maintain a spreadsheet recording your purchases and sales and you keep your buy and sell contract notes in an orderly manner (see chapters 3 and 9). Your share trades are properly accounted for (namely: sales – cost of goods sold – deductible expenses = net profit).

- *Whether you maintain an office.* For instance, you hire out an office or you have set aside a room at your home specifically to conduct your share trading transactions.

- *Whether you are trading on a full-time or part-time basis.* Under Australian tax law a person can carry on a business in a small way. Although there are no specific rules to say you can't trade on a part-time basis, it will strengthen your argument that you're carrying on a share trading business if you do it on a full-time basis.

- *Whether you have a full-time profession.* There are no rules to say that if you have a full-time profession you can't carry on a share trading business at the same time; for instance, you do your research after work hours or at weekends, and you conduct your trading activities during your lunch break. But again, it will strengthen your argument that you're carrying on a share trading business if you do not have another full-time profession.

Although it's not necessary for you to satisfy every single test (for instance, you do not maintain an office and you have a full-time profession as a bricklayer), the overall evidence (impression) must clearly indicate that your activities are similar to that of a share trader carrying on a share trading business.

Generally speaking it's relatively easy to satisfy these key tests. But you'll generally find the stumbling block as to whether you'll be classified as a share trader for tax purposes is satisfying the test associated with 'the frequency of trades you do each year'. This is because a genuine share trader will normally carry out regular and repetitive trades over a long period of time, with the prime objective to make a profit (for instance, between 5 and 10 trades per week). A share investor's trading pattern, on the other hand, would tend to be less frequent and irregular. Share investors will tend to hold their shares over a longer period of time, with the prime intention of receiving regular dividend payments and possibly long-term capital growth.

Case study: carrying on a share trading business

Ralph is a full-time farmer who is very eager to make a lot of money trading on the stock market. He has undertaken a number of training courses, has a $40000 budget to finance his share trading transactions, and has a $20000 bank overdraft in case he needs additional funds. He has a computer, access to the internet and has set up an account with an online stockbroker. Each morning he reads the financial newspapers to assess which companies to buy, and watches the dedicated business television channels to keep up to date with current trends. He also subscribes to stock market newsletters prepared by stockbrokers. He normally does at least one trade at the beginning of each day. His plan is to sell them if they rise more than 5 per cent in value or fall more than 3 per cent in value. Over the past nine months he has conducted over 200 trades and has managed to make a $7000 profit. He has recorded all his trades on a spreadsheet and has kept his buy and sell contract notes in an orderly manner. He has also set aside a room at his home to conduct his share trading activities.

Although Ralph is a full-time farmer carrying on his share trading activities on a part-time basis, the facts indicate:

⇛ he has an intention of making a profit from his share trading activities

⇛ he is carrying on his activities in a businesslike manner

⇛ his activities are regular and repetitive

⇛ the number of trades he has performed is very high

⇛ he has a budget to fund his share trading transactions and has a trading strategy in place

⇛ he maintains proper records

⇛ he has set aside a room to conduct his share trading activities.

Ralph would be considered to be carrying on a business as a share trader. The overall evidence (impression) clearly indicates that Ralph's activities are similar to that of a genuine share trader.

This means:

⇒ all his sales are treated as assessable income

⇒ all his purchases are tax deductible expenses

⇒ he will need to bring to account stock on hand at the end of the financial year (namely, shares not yet sold)

⇒ he can claim expenditure necessarily incurred in carrying on a business for the purposes of gaining assessable income (see chapter 5).

 Tax trap

If you're on the borderline or you're not sure whether you are a share trader or share investor; don't guess. Tax penalties could apply if you get it wrong and you could find yourself paying more tax than is necessary. You should seek professional advice from a registered tax agent or get a private ruling from the ATO as to whether your profits (or losses) should be taxed on revenue account or under the CGT provisions. Incidentally, if you plan to apply for a private ruling the ATO has prepared a publication *Private rulings and advice essentials*. You can download a copy from the Tax Office website and read the section 'Are you carrying on a business? (Supporting document requirements for private rulings)'. You will need to address the key tests mentioned in the previous section, as this will determine whether you are carrying on a business as a share trader or you are a share investor.

Share trader

If you're classified as a share trader you don't need to apply for an Australian Business Number (ABN), or quote this number to a stockbroker at the time they buy and sell your shares on the Australian Securities Exchange. With respect to your share trading activities you will need to do the following:

- Apply for a tax file number (TFN) and quote this number whenever you contact the ATO or lodge your annual tax return disclosing your share trading activities. Incidentally, you are not legally obligated to supply your TFN to a stockbroker when you buy or sell your shares.

- You may need to prepare a business activity statement or instalment activity statement disclosing your share trading profits and dividends, and pay tax on a monthly or quarterly basis. The Tax Office will inform you whether you'll need to do this. This means you'll need to keep an accurate record of all your share transactions on an ongoing basis.

- At the end of the financial year (30 June) you must prepare a profit and loss statement disclosing the net profit you derived (or net loss you incurred) from your share trading activities. To do this correctly you'll need to read the Tax Office publication *Business and professional items* and complete the *Business and professional items schedule for individuals*.

- You will need to insert your trading results at Item 15: Net income or loss from business, located in your tax return for individuals (supplementary section).

- Any dividends you derive must be disclosed at Item 12: Dividends, located in your tax return for individuals.

Share investor

If you are a share investor you will need to apply for a TFN and quote this number whenever you contact the ATO or lodge your annual tax return for individuals. You may also need to quote your TFN to a particular company at the time you buy your shares, otherwise the company may withhold tax from your dividend payments. This will normally occur if a company pays you an unfranked dividend. For more details see the Tax Office publication *Reporting withholding and investment income payments* (NAT 15073). With respect to your share transactions you will need to do the following:

- Any dividends and franking credits you receive must be disclosed at Item 12: Dividends, located in your tax return for individuals. Incidentally, if tax was withheld from your dividend payments because you did not quote your TFN to the company, you will need to insert the amount of tax withheld at Item 12 (V): Tax file number amounts withheld from dividends.

- Any tax deductible expenses must be disclosed at Item D7: Interest and dividends, located in your tax return for individuals. For more details see chapter 5.

- Any capital gains and capital losses must be disclosed at Item 18: Capital gains, located in your tax return for individuals (supplementary section).

- You may be required to prepare an instalment activity statement disclosing the dividends you derive and pay tax on an ongoing basis (normally on a quarterly basis). The Tax Office will inform you whether you'll need to do this. Incidentally, you are not required to disclose any capital gains you make, franking credits you receive, or any expenses you incur in respect of your dividend payments. For more details see Tax Office publication *PAYG instalments—how to complete your activity statement*.

Case study: share trader

Four years ago Brooke, who is a school teacher, contacted her stockbroker and purchased a $150 000 quality blue chip share portfolio that pays franked dividends. Over the years she has been steadily accumulating high dividend-yielding companies and has sold some companies that were not performing to her satisfaction. Last year she received $7500 dividends and incurred $3000 interest on borrowings to finance her purchases. She also sold a parcel of shares she held for three years and made a $35000 capital gain.

As Brooke had purchased the shares for the purposes of gaining dividends rather than to make a profit on sale, she is considered to be a share investor. This means:

⇒ The $7500 dividends are assessable.

⇒ The $3000 interest on borrowings is a tax deductible expense, as it was incurred in the course of gaining assessable income (dividends).

⇒ The $35000 capital gain on sale is liable to tax under the CGT provisions. As the shares were held for more than 12 months, only 50 per cent of the capital gain is liable to tax. The balance is exempt and excluded from assessable income (see chapter 6).

Share trader versus share investor

The reason a person would be eager to be classified as a share trader for tax purposes is your capacity to claim any trading losses you incur as a tax deductible expense. As mentioned previously, share traders can claim certain expenditures that are not readily available to a share investor. The trade-off is a share trader is unable to claim a 50 per cent CGT discount on shares held for more than 12 months. But this is unlikely to be of any major concern, as a genuine share trader is unlikely to hold their shares for any significant period of time.

 Tax tip

If you are a share trader it's possible for you to hold certain shares as trading stock that you intend to trade for the purposes of making a profit, and shares you intend to hold for investment purposes (for instance, to derive regular dividends and long-term capital growth). You'll need to separate your share holdings and keep proper records to make this distinction quite clear (for instance, you record the details in a CGT asset register; see chapter 9).

Checklist: share trader versus share investor

Let's take a look at how you are taxed under Australian tax law.

Income

Share trading sales and realised capital gains are taxable in the financial year they are derived. Share traders will be aiming to make a quick profit from each trade they enter into; for instance, buy in the morning and immediately sell them if they increase in value. All proceeds from sale are treated as assessable income for tax purposes. The income is ordinarily recognised when received. A share investor would tend to hold their shares for the dominant purpose of deriving regular dividend payments and long-term capital growth (rather than to make a quick profit on sale). All dividends are assessable and all profits on sale are treated as capital gains for tax purposes.

Losses

A major benefit of being classified as a share trader is all trading losses and outgoings can be deducted from other assessable income you derive (for instance, salary and wages, business profits and investment income). This will allow you to immediately recoup any trading losses and expenses you incur. So it's important that you have another source of income to offset your trading losses. Keep in mind no tax is payable once your taxable income falls below $16 000 (per 2010–11 tax rates), so you could lose this significant benefit if your losses are substantial and your assessable income from other sources is minimal. Incidentally, business losses can be carried forward to the next financial year. In contrast, if you are a share investor any loss you incur is classified as a capital loss. Under the CGT provisions, a capital loss is quarantined and can only be offset against a capital gain.

Trading stock

If you carry on a share trading business, at the end of the financial year you'll need to bring to account shares not yet sold as trading stock on hand. So you'll need to do the following:

- You can value your trading stock on hand at cost or market value on a share-by-share basis. The term 'cost' means the price you paid for your shares while 'market value' is the market price of your shares as at the close of trading on 30 June. It's therefore possible for you to take full advantage of any unrealised losses you may incur at the end of the financial year. For example, on 29 June your share purchases were $40 000 and on 30 June the market price had fallen to $25 000. The $15 000 decrease in value can be claimed as a tax deduction.

- The closing value of your trading stock on hand on 30 June must be the same as the opening value of your trading stock at the beginning of the next financial year (namely, 1 July).

On the other hand, if you are a share investor you don't need to do this because you're only required to bring to account your realised capital gains and capital losses.

 Tax tip

For a comprehensive discussion on valuing shares see income tax ruling TR 96/4 *Income tax: valuing shares acquired as revenue assets.* You can get a copy from your local ATO or you can visit its website.

Purchase costs

If you are a share trader your purchase costs (for instance, brokerage and GST) are tax deductible expenses and can be claimed in the financial year they're incurred. If you are a share investor your purchase costs will form part of the cost base of your share purchases, and can only be taken into account when calculating a capital gain or capital loss on disposal. Incidentally, no GST is payable on share transactions as they are classified as input taxed. But you're liable to pay GST on your brokerage fees.

Deductible expenses

If you are a share trader you can depreciate your computer and claim home office expenses and other expenses associated with carrying on a share trading business (for instance, your contributions to a complying superannuation fund may qualify as a tax deductible expense). Share investors, on the other hand, can only claim certain expenses associated with deriving dividends. So it's important that the shares you buy pay dividends, otherwise you could miss out. For more details see chapter 5.

CGT discount

A major limitation of being classified as a share trader is your inability of claim the 50 per cent CGT discount in respect of shares held for more than 12 months (as is the case if you are a share investor). As share traders are unlikely to hold their shares for more than 12 months, it's unlikely that this situation will arise.

Useful references

- Tax Case: 'Shields v Deputy Federal Commissioner of Taxation': Issue: carrying on a share trading business over a short period of time; claiming share trading losses.

Australian Taxation Office publications

- *Carrying on a business of share trading*
- *Claiming losses from the disposal of investments*
- *Holding shares or actively trading: what's the difference?*
- *Investments, shares and options essentials*
- *Losses from earlier years*
- *Record keeping for small business* (NAT 3029)
- *Sale of shares (Supporting document requirements for private rulings)*
- *Tax basics for small business* (NAT 1908)

Australian Taxation Office interpretative decisions

- ID 2001/746: *Shares and securities trading*
- ID 2010/52: *Income tax: deductions and expenses: short sale transactions and securities lending arrangements*

Other taxation rulings

- **TA 2009/12:** *Re-characterising capital losses as revenue losses*

- **TR 97/7:** *Income tax: section 8-1—meaning of 'incurred'—timing of deductions*

- **TR 97/11:** *Income tax: am I carrying on a business of primary production?*

- **TR 98/1:** *Determination of income; receipts versus earnings*

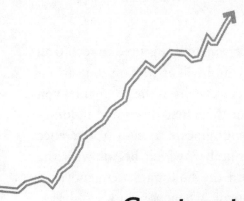

Chapter 3

Contract notes: the foundations of your taxation records

There are two different ways you can hold shares listed on the Australian Securities Exchange: broker-sponsored under CHESS (Clearing House Electronic Subregister System) or issuer-sponsored. In this chapter I explain how these two methods operate and look at the record-keeping issues when you use a stockbroker to buy and sell shares on your behalf.

Under the broker-sponsored method you will need to sign a sponsorship agreement with your stockbroker. If you do this your stockbroker will issue a holder identification number (HIN) that begins with the letter 'X' and will become your identification number on the

CHESS system. Your personal HIN is used to record all your share transactions, and will appear on the various holding statements you receive from the companies you own shares with. Under the issuer-sponsored holdings option the company will allocate a security reference number (SRN). This number, which begins with the letter 'I', is recorded on the holding statement you'll receive from the company when you buy its shares. So if you purchase shares in different companies you will be issued with their respective security reference numbers.

Transaction costs and tax

When a stockbroker buys and sells a parcel of shares on your behalf you are liable to pay a brokerage fee and GST. Brokerage fees can vary from between 0.4 per cent and 1.5 per cent of the purchase or sale price. The GST component is 10 per cent of your brokerage fees. So if your brokerage fees are $100 the GST payable is $10. The way you will account for your transaction costs for tax purposes will depend on whether you are carrying on a business as a share trader or you're a share investor. In chapter 2 it was pointed out if you are a share trader your brokerage fees and GST are tax deductible expenses (being a part of the cost of trading operations). These expenses are tax deductible in the financial year they are incurred. On the other hand, if you are a share investor your brokerage fees and GST are not tax deductible. Under the capital gains tax (CGT) provisions they will form part of the cost base of your shares. This means they can only be taken into account when calculating whether you have made a capital gain or capital loss on disposal (see chapter 6). But when it all boils down this is merely a timing adjustment as to when you can recognise your *purchase* transaction costs as a tax deductible expense; for share investors this will happen when the shares are sold (rather than when they're incurred if you are a share trader).

Tax tip

Under the GST provisions share transactions are input taxed. This means no GST is levied on your share transactions. But you will be liable to pay GST in respect of the brokerage fees your stockbroker will charge you.

Buy contract notes

When a stockbroker buys shares on your behalf you will receive a buy contract note (or invoice). If you perform the transaction online you will normally receive this document as soon as the buy order is executed. Your stockbroker will immediately forward a buy contact note to you by mail and full payment must be made by the settlement day. This document will set out the full details of the transaction and will become your core document for record-keeping purposes (see figure 3.1, overleaf).

Figure 3.1: buy contract note

BUY
Contract Note
Stockbrokers United

Eddy Simpson
52 Greenwood Street
Greenwood NSW

Tax Invoice

We have bought the following securities for you

Company: Apex Ltd
Security: Ordinary Fully Paid

Date:	21 July 20XX
Contract Number:	42697401
Account No:	69421076
Total Units:	1000
Cost Price:	$15.45
Consideration (AUD):	$15 450.00
Brokerage & costs including GST:	$100.00
Total Cost:	$15 550.00
Settlement Date:	24 July 20XX

The buy contract note will set out information such as:

- *Total units:* as a matter of course you should always check that the number of shares you purchased (total units) agrees with the holding statement you will receive from the company (see figure 3.2, p. 41).

- *Contract number:* the contract number can be used to help you keep track of the shares you purchased. Complications can arise if you buy different parcels in the same company on different occasions and sell them at a later date. This is because under the CGT provisions each parcel you buy is treated as a separate CGT asset with its own cost base and purchase date. So you'll need to be able to identify the individual shares within a holding of identical shares. Fortunately the contract number can help you overcome this problem when calculating whether you have made a capital gain or capital loss. For more details see chapters 6 and 9.

- *Date of purchase:* ordinarily you're considered to have acquired the shares on the date of purchase (being the date of the making of the contract). This becomes an important date when working out whether you had held your shares for at least 12 months. If this is the case you can claim a 50 per cent CGT discount if you make a capital gain. For more details see chapter 6.

- *Purchase price:* if you are a share trader this is a tax deductible expense. If you are a share investor under the CGT provisions this will become part of the cost base of your shares.

- *Purchase costs (brokerages and GST):* as mentioned in the previous section, if you are a share trader these can be claimed as tax deductible expenses (being part of the cost of trading operations) in the financial year they are incurred. Conversely, if you are a share investor, under the CGT provisions these costs are included as part of the cost base of your shares.

If you are a share trader you should immediately record all your purchase details on a spreadsheet in strict date order as illustrated in table 3.1. This will help you to quickly calculate the amount you incurred when preparing your tax return.

Table 3.1: summary of purchases

Purchase date	Total outlay	Deductible purchase price	Deductible brokerage & GST	Company name	Total units	Contract number
21 July 20XX	$15 550.00	$15 450.00	$100.00	Apex Ltd	1000	42697401

If you are a share investor you should record the buy contract note details in strict date order on a spreadsheet as set out in chapter 9, figure 9.2: summary of share transactions (pp. 182–183). You should also keep a record of each individual company you hold shares in as set out in chapter 9, figure 9.3: record of share holdings (p. 184). This will help you to quickly work out whether you have made a capital gain or capital loss when the shares are sold (as illustrated in figure 9.3).

A few weeks after you buy your shares the company will issue a holding statement, confirming proof of ownership and the number of shares you currently hold in the company. Incidentally, since 1998 listed companies no longer issue share certificates to its shareholders. When you examine your holding statement you'll find it will merely record the number of shares you currently own in the company and nothing more (see figure 3.2). So it's important that you keep your holding statement with the corresponding buy contact note. If you misplace your buy contract note you can get a duplicate copy from your stockbroker.

Figure 3.2: holding statement

Apex Ltd	
Eddy Simpson	
52 Greenwood Street	
Greenwood NSW	
Holder Identification Number (HIN)	
X 00628903482	
Security class:	Ordinary fully paid shares
Holding Statement as at 8 August 20XX	
Date	8 August 20XX
Transaction Type	Transfer
Opening Balance	0
Quantity On	1000
Quantity Off	
Holding Balance	1000

Sell contract notes

As soon as your stockbroker executes a sell order on your behalf you will receive a sell contract note setting out the details of sale (see figure 3.3, overleaf). At the time of sale you may need to quote either your HIN or SRN to your stockbroker to verify that the number of shares you sold matches the company's share register records. You will normally get your money back (less brokerage fees and GST) within a few days of selling them. The company will then send you an amended holding statement verifying the number of shares you had sold.

Figure 3.3: sell contract note

SELL
Contract Note
Stockbrokers United

Eddy Simpson
52 Greenwood Street
Greenwood NSW

Tax Invoice

- -

We have sold the following securities for you
Company: Apex Ltd
Security: Ordinary Fully Paid

- -

Date:	18 October 20XX
Contract Number	84192367
Account No.	69421076
Total Units:	1000
Sale Price:	$21.50
Consideration (AUD):	$21 500.00
Brokerage & costs including GST:	$100.00
Net Proceeds:	$21 400.00
Settlement Date	21 October 20XX

If you are a share trader the gross proceeds from sale will be returned as part of your assessable income and the brokerage and GST payable is a tax deductible expense. The income is ordinarily recognised when you receive the payment. You should record each sale you make in strict date order on a spreadsheet (as illustrated in table 3.2). Conversely, if you are a share investor you will need to work out whether you have made a capital gain or capital loss (see chapters 6 and 9). This will arise at the time of sale (being the date the contract was made).

Table 3.2: summary of sales

Sale date	Assessable gross sales	Deductible brokerage & GST	Net sale price	Company name	Total units	Contract number
18 Oct 20XX	$21 500.00	$100.00	$21 400.00	Apex Ltd	1000	84192367

 Tax tip

If you buy and sell shares within the same financial year and you make a profit on sale, the taxable profit (if you are a share trader) or capital gain (if you are a share investor) is identical. This is because if you are a share investor you will be effectively claiming the brokerage and GST you'll incur as if they were tax deductible expenses.

Useful references

- Australian Securities Exchange website <www.asx.com.au> — go to:
  - 'Shares' then click on 'Buy and sell'
  - Frequently asked questions about CHESS.

CHAPTER 4

Taxation and ownership structures

There are six main ways you can own shares. In this chapter I examine these options and look at the tax issues that could influence your decision as to which one is right for you. The six different ownership structures you can consider are:

- individual ownership

- joint ownership

- managed funds (share trusts)

- company

- trust

- self managed superannuation funds.

Tax trap

When you buy shares you're not legally required to quote your tax file number (TFN) to the company. But if a TFN is not provided, the company will withhold tax at the rate of 46.5 per cent from any unfranked dividends it pays you. You can claim this back when you lodge your annual tax return. See chapter 2 for more details.

Individual ownership

If you buy shares in your name you will own them outright. This means you will need to declare all the dividend payments and franking credits you receive and any capital gains you make in your individual tax return. Further, any expenditure you incur in the course of deriving your dividends (for instance, interest on borrowings) is a tax deductible expense (see chapter 5). And if you receive a franked dividend you can claim a dividend franking tax offset. You'll need to disclose the following information in your tax return for individuals:

- All franked dividends and unfranked dividends and franking credits must be disclosed at Item 12: Dividends.

- Capital gains and capital losses you make must be disclosed in your tax return for individuals (supplementary section) at Item 18: Capital gains.

- Expenditure you incur in deriving your dividend income must be disclosed at Item D7: Interest and dividend deductions.

If you carry on a business as a share trader you will need to insert your trading results at Item 15: Net income or loss from business, which is located in your tax return for individuals (supplementary section) — see chapter 2 for more details.

At a glance: how individuals are taxed

This is how an individual is taxed under Australian tax law:

- Individuals must apply for a tax file number (TFN) and quote this number when they lodge their individual tax return.

- Individuals may need to quote their TFN to a company if the company is likely to pay unfranked dividends. If no TFN is quoted the company will withhold tax at the rate of 46.5 per cent. You can claim this back when you lodge your tax return for individuals at Item 12 (V): Tax file number amounts withheld from dividends.

- Individuals are liable to pay tax at their marginal rates of tax (which can vary between 0 per cent and 45 per cent).

- Individuals are entitled to a $6000 tax-free threshold.

- No tax is payable if your taxable income falls below $16000 (per 2010–11 tax rates).

- Individuals are liable to pay a 1.5 per cent Medicare levy.

- Individuals can claim domestic tax offsets (such as a dividend franking credit tax offset, a low income tax offset and a senior Australians tax offset).

- Individuals can claim a 50 per cent CGT discount in respect of any capital gains on disposal of CGT assets (such as shares) owned for more than 12 months (see chapter 5).

- Individuals can only offset their capital losses against capital gains. If you make no capital gains, the capital loss can be offset against future capital gains (see chapter 5).

Limitations

A major limitation of outright ownership is you can't split your dividend payments and capital gains and capital losses with family members (for instance, with your partner or children). Under the CGT provisions, if you transfer or gift your shares to someone else (or to your self managed superannuation fund) there will be a change of ownership. This means you could be liable to pay CGT on any capital gain you make at the time you transfer your shares.

Shares in the name of a child

In Australia a child (or minor) is a person who is under the age of 18. Ordinarily a child who earns less than $3333 (per 2010–11 tax rates) is not required to lodge a tax return for individuals disclosing the taxable income they derive. But a tax return will need to be lodged if tax was withheld or the child is entitled to a refund of any dividend franking credits.

If a child owns shares in their own name they may need to quote a TFN to the company. This is because if no TFN is quoted the company must withhold 46.5 per cent tax if the dividend payment is unfranked. There is no withholding threshold for dividends (as is the case with interest derived by a child). If the shares are purchased in the name of the child with the parent as trustee, the parent will need to quote their individual TFN to the company. But if a formal trust is in place you'll need to quote the trust's TFN to the company.

According to the Tax Office rulings, whoever rightly owns and controls the shares must declare the dividends and any capital gains on sale. The Tax Office has provided examples to clarify who must declare dividends and capital gains in respect of shares in the name of a child, for instance:

- If a person (for instance, parent) uses their own money to buy shares in the child's name and deposits the dividends in their own account, and uses the funds for their own purposes, the dividend should be assessed to that person.

- If a person (for instance, parent) uses their own money to buy shares in the child's name and deposits the dividends (and any capital gains on sale) in the child's account, the dividends (and capital gains) must be declared in the child's tax return.

- If a person uses money a child had saved from a part-time job (plus any money received for a child's birthday) to buy shares in the child's name, and deposits dividends (and any capital gains on sale) in the child's account, the dividends (and capital gains) must be declared in the child's tax return.

 Tax tip

The Tax Office uses the following terms to describe how income derived by a child is liable to be taxed:

⇒ *Eligible income*: this is unearned income derived by a child that was not earned through their own efforts (for instance, dividends derived from a family discretionary trust). This income is liable to tax at a special rate as set out in table 4.1: distribution to minors: special rate of tax (p. 59).

⇒ *Excepted income*: this is income a child earned through their own efforts (for instance, from working at a fast-food outlet). So if a child were to invest this money to derive dividends, the dividends will be treated as excepted assessable income. This income is liable to tax at the child's marginal rates of tax. You will need to insert this amount at Item A1: Under 18, in the child's tax return for individuals. This is to avoid paying a special rate of tax on this amount.

For more details you can read Tax Office publications *Children's share investments* and *Refund of franking credit instructions and application for individuals*. See also taxation determination TD 93/148: *Income tax: are monetary gifts received by a child or any interest earned on investing such money treated as 'excepted assessable income'?*

Joint ownership

Under Australian tax law persons in receipt of income jointly are considered to be in partnership. Owning shares in joint names (for instance, husband and wife) is similar to owning them outright, but you can split the dividends and franking credits you receive and any capital gains and capital losses you make among the joint owners. You must do this in accordance with their legal entitlement (usually on a 50–50 basis). Further, you can claim your share of any expenditure you incur in deriving your dividend payments (for instance, interest on borrowings to buy jointly owned shares). A major advantage of a partnership (and more particularly joint names) arrangement is a partnership can access partnership losses (especially capital losses). This is not the case if the shares are held in a company or trust structure.

At a glance: how joint ownership of shares is taxed

This is how a partnership is taxed under Australian tax law:

- A partnership is not liable to pay tax on the net income it derives. Instead, all income and losses must be distributed to the individual partners.

- If you are in receipt of income jointly you don't need to apply for a partnership TFN or lodge a partnership tax return. However, you will need to disclose your share of any dividends and franking credits, capital gains and capital losses, and tax deductible expenses in your tax return for individuals (see section Individual Ownership).

Limitations

A major limitation of owning shares jointly is your inability to distribute all the dividends and capital gains to one joint owner who may stand to benefit the most (for instance, to the person who pays the least amount of tax). Nor can one joint owner claim all the tax deductions or all the capital losses. All distributions must be made in accordance with each owner's legal entitlement to that distribution. This is normally done on a 50–50 basis unless you can prove otherwise (for instance, on a 75–25 basis if you contribute 75 per cent of the funds and your partner contributes 25 per cent).

Managed funds (share trusts)

Managed funds (and more particularly share trusts) are mutual investment funds managed by Australia's leading financial institutions (such as banks and insurance companies). They give individual investors the opportunity to invest in domestic and foreign listed companies. A major benefit of this way of investing is you can select an appropriate share portfolio mix to meet your particular needs. It will also give you the opportunity to invest in various listed public companies that may be out of your price range. The asset classes in which you can invest include:

- *Equity growth:* where your money is invested in a share portfolio of Australian and international listed companies.

- *Foreign:* where your money is invested in major international companies (for instance the United States, Europe and Asia).

- *Indexed:* where your money is invested in a particular index (such as the S&P/ASX 200 index comprising the top 200 companies listed on the Australian Securities Exchange).

Under this arrangement you will not own the shares outright. Rather, you'll be issued with units. The value of your units is market-linked, meaning they will rise and fall in line with the prevailing sharemarket. This could prove a good way of investing in the sharemarket if you're inexperienced or would prefer someone to manage your share portfolio for you. Managed funds normally distribute assessable income (such as dividends and franking credits) every six months. You could also receive non-assessable amounts where you may need to adjust the cost base and reduced cost base of your units (see Tax Office publication *Non-assessable payments*). If you sell your units you could be liable to pay CGT if they had appreciated in value. Any assessable distributions will need to be disclosed in your tax return for individuals (supplementary section) at Item 13: Partnerships and trusts, and you are liable to pay tax at your marginal rates of tax (plus Medicare levy). For a comprehensive discussion on the taxation of managed funds you can read Tax Office publication *Personal investors guide to capital gains tax* (NAT 4152).

Limitations

Two major limitations of this way of investing are you will incur ongoing fees to manage your investment portfolio, and your inability to choose specific companies in which to buy shares.

Company structure

In chapter 1 it was pointed out that a company is a separate legal entity. This means it can own assets such as shares in its own right and must apply for a TFN and lodge an annual company tax return. Under Australian tax law a company pays a 30 per cent rate of tax on the net profit it derives. (At the time of writing, the Federal Labor Government has proposed to reduce the company tax rate to 29 per cent in the 2013–14 financial year and to 28 per cent in the 2014–15 financial year.) A major benefit of setting up and investing in a company structure is it doesn't have to distribute dividends to shareholders. The profit can remain within the company structure and you can choose when to make a dividend distribution.

Limitations

There are numerous restrictions or conditions associated with buying shares in a company structure (especially if you set up a private company) that may not be to your advantage. The main ones are set out here:

- Company profits derived from all sources (for instance, investment income, exempt profits and capital gains) are taxed as dividends when distributed to shareholders. And you will receive a franking credit if the dividends are franked. Incidentally, the company must maintain a 'franking account' to record franking debits and franking credits. For more details see Tax Office publication *Simplified imputation—the franking account*.

 Tax trap

Ordinarily payments (or transfer of property) made by a private company to a shareholder or an associate of a shareholder (for instance, a relative) are treated as unfranked dividends. For more details see Tax Office publication *You and your shares— transactions that will be treated as dividends* (NAT 2632).

- A company can't stream dividend payments to specific shareholders. Dividend distributions must be made in proportion to the number of shares each shareholder owns. For example, if you own 50 per cent of the shares in a company you will receive 50 per cent of the dividend distributions and franking credits.

- A company cannot distribute company losses to shareholders. This will be the case whether you are carrying on a share trading business or you are a share investor. These losses must remain within the company and can only be deducted from future company profits. Incidentally, if you set up a private company (which will most likely be the case) you will need to satisfy complex tax rules to access losses incurred in earlier years. For more details see Tax Office publication *Guide to the loss recoupment rules*.

- A company is ineligible to claim a 50 per cent CGT discount on capital gains made on disposal of shares owned for more than 12 months. This could be a major disincentive to maintaining an investment share portfolio in a company structure, especially if you're planning to hold shares for the long term.

- Companies miss out on the $6000 tax-free threshold which is available to individual share investors. Companies effectively pay a 30 per cent rate of tax on the entire net profit they derive from all sources.

Tax trap

If a shareholder receives an unsecured loan from a private company, there are anti–tax avoidance provisions to treat the amount as an unfranked dividend in the financial year the payment is made. This could arise if there is no written commercial loan agreement setting out minimum yearly repayments and/or no benchmark interest rate. For more details see Tax Office publication *Division 7A essentials*.

 Tax tip

If you operate a small business in a company structure and you sell your shares in the company, you could qualify for the small business CGT concessions if you satisfy a 20 per cent significant individual test. This test checks whether an individual has at least a 20 per cent small business participation percentage with respect to:

⇒ the voting power an individual can exercise in running the business

⇒ entitlement to receive dividend distributions the business makes

⇒ entitlement to receive capital distributions the business makes.

For more details see Tax Office publication *Significant individual test—fact sheet*.

Trust structure

One popular way of owning investments and more particularly a share portfolio is to set up a trust. A trust is a legal obligation binding a person (the trustee) who has control over investment assets (for instance, a share portfolio) for the benefit of beneficiaries. If you set up a family discretionary trust, the trustee has discretion as to how the trust net income (for instance, dividends and capital gains) should be distributed to the beneficiaries (normally family members). A major advantage of investing in a trust structure is the trustee can select which beneficiaries should receive a trust distribution (which is not the case if the investments are held in a company structure). For instance, as no tax is payable once your taxable income is below $16000 (per 2010–11 tax rates), a trustee could effectively distribute only to adult beneficiaries whose taxable income is below this amount.

Limitations

The limitations from investing in a trust structure are as follows:

- There are anti–tax avoidance provisions to discourage trustees from distributing 'unearned income' such as dividend payments to beneficiaries under the age of 18. Distributions to minor beneficiaries are taxed at a special rate (see table 4.1). As minor beneficiaries can claim a low income tax offset, they can effectively receive up to $3333 (per 2010–11 tax rates) before this special rate of tax will apply.

- A trust cannot distribute losses (and more particularly capital losses) to beneficiaries. These losses must remain within the trust structure and can only be offset against future trust income. There are also complex rules you'll have to comply with to claim trust losses. For more details see Tax Office publication *Trust losses*.

Table 4.1: distribution to minors: special rate of tax

Taxable income	Rate of tax
$0–$416	Nil tax payable
$417–$1307	66% of excess over $416
Above $1307	45% on entire amount of taxable income

 Tax tip

Income flowing through a trust will retain its identity or character when a trustee makes a distribution to beneficiaries. What this means is if the trustee distributes a franked dividend or a capital gain that qualifies for a 50 per cent CGT discount, it will be a franked dividend or a capital gain that qualifies for a 50 per cent CGT discount in the hands of the beneficiaries. This is not the case if a distribution is made by a company because companies can only distribute dividends to shareholders.

At a glance: how trusts are taxed

This is how a trust is taxed under Australian tax law:

- The trustee must apply for a TFN and lodge a trust return disclosing the trust net income.

- The trust is not liable to pay tax on the trust net income it derives. The income is assessed to either the trustee or beneficiaries. Under trust law, once the trustee has calculated the trust net income, the trustee must ascertain:

  - who the beneficiaries are

  - whether any beneficiary is 'presently entitled' to receive a trust distribution

  - whether any beneficiary is 'under a legal disability' (for instance, under 18 years of age).

- If a beneficiary is presently entitled to receive a trust distribution (meaning they have a legal right to demand payment), the income is assessed to them. The beneficiary will need to include the amount as part of their assessable income in their tax return for individuals (supplementary section) at Item 13: Partnerships and trusts. The amount they receive is liable to tax at their marginal rates of tax (plus Medicare levy), and they can claim franking credits if the dividends are franked.

- If a beneficiary is presently entitled but is under a legal disability (for instance, a child under 18 years of age), the trustee is liable to pay the tax and can claim any franking credits.

■ If no beneficiary is presently entitled or the trustee decides not to make a distribution, the trustee is ordinarily liable to pay tax at the rate of 46.5 per cent and can claim any franking credits.

Case study: receiving a trust distribution

According to the accounts of the DEF family discretionary trust the trust received the following amounts from its share portfolio:

Dividends	$17 500
Franking credits	$7 500
Net trust income	$25 000

At the end of the financial year the trustee resolved to distribute the trust net income to the following beneficiaries:

⇒ $14 286 (includes $4286 franking credit) to Lisa, who is 19 years of age and in full-time education.

⇒ $7857 (includes $2357 franking credit) to Margaret, who is 21 years of age and in full-time education. She also derived salary and wages totalling $8000.

⇒ $2857 (includes $857 franking credit) to Nathan, who is six years of age.

Distribution to Lisa ($14 286)

As Lisa is over 18 years of age she is presently entitled to the trust distribution and is under no legal disability. She is personally liable to pay tax on this amount and can claim a franking credit. As her taxable income is below $16 000 no tax is payable. The Tax Office will refund the $4286 franking credits to her.

Distribution to Margaret ($7857)

As Margaret is over 18 years of age she is presently entitled to the trust distribution and is under no legal disability. She is personally liable to pay tax on this amount and can claim a franking credit. Her total taxable income is $15 857 ($7857 plus $8000). No tax is payable as her taxable income is below $16 000. The Tax Office will refund the $2357 franking credits to her.

Distribution to Nathan ($2857)

As Nathan is presently entitled to the trust distribution but is under a legal disability (a beneficiary under 18 years of age), the trustee is liable to pay tax on this distribution. As the amount distributed was less than $3333, no tax is payable and the Tax Office will refund the $857 franking credits to the trustee. This is because a minor beneficiary can claim a low-income tax offset.

Self managed superannuation funds

A self managed superannuation fund (SMSF) is a super fund that you can manage and run yourself. It will allow you to accumulate wealth-creation investments like shares to help you fund your own retirement. A significant advantage of running an SMSF is you can choose your own investment strategy to build wealth (for instance, a quality share portfolio paying fully franked dividends). There are many taxation benefits to encourage you to put money into a complying SMSF. Incidentally, it's called a complying fund because you must elect to be regulated (for instance, by the Australian Taxation Office) within 60 days of setting up your fund, if you want to gain these tax benefits.

 Tax trap

If you intend to set up an SMSF you will have to prepare an 'investment strategy' setting out how you intend to invest your funds (for instance, in the sharemarket) and the risks associated with the investment. For more details see Tax Office publication *Investment strategy*.

At a glance: how complying superannuation funds are taxed

This is how a complying superannuation fund is taxed under Australian tax law:

- A complying super fund is liable to pay tax at the rate of 15 per cent. But your fund's tax liability could be reduced to nil if you receive fully franked dividends. Any excess franking credits are refunded to your fund (see Case study: taxing your SMSF, p. 65).

- If your super fund owns shares for more than 12 months, only two-thirds of any capital gain your fund makes is liable to tax at the rate of 15 per cent. This means the entire capital gain is effectively taxed at the rate of 10 per cent.

- Pensions payable once you turn 60 years of age are exempt from tax (see Case study: receiving a superannuation pension, p. 66).

- Any income and capital gains your fund derives to fund your pension payments are exempt from tax, which means all dividend franking credits will be refunded to your super fund.

- There are tax incentives to encourage you to make a contribution to a super fund. For instance, if you're self-employed your contributions are tax deductible, and you can use these funds to build up a quality share portfolio.

 Tax trap

A major limitation of an SMSF is your inability to access your accumulated benefits until you reach your preservation age and retire. If you're born before 1960 you can access your benefits once you reach 55 years of age, or at 60 years of age if you're born after 1964.

A major advantage of setting up an SMSF is you can transfer 'listed securities' (such as your personal share portfolio) to your super fund. Be aware that if you do this you'll be effectively selling your shares to your super fund, which means you could be liable to pay capital gains tax if the shares you transfer had increased in value.

 Tax trap

If you own shares in a self managed superannuation fund you cannot benefit from any discounts a company may offer its shareholders. This is because you will be considered to have breached the sole purpose test, as you cannot benefit from your super fund until you satisfy a condition of release (for instance, you retire). For more details see Self managed superannuation funds ruling SMSFR 2008/2.

Case study: taxing your SMSF

At the end of the financial year the accounts of your SMSF provided the following details:

Dividends fully franked	$30 000
Dividend franking credits	$12 857
Audit and accounting fees	$1 000

Superannuation fund tax return

How your SMSF is taxed is shown overleaf.

Taxable income

Dividends	$30 000
Dividend franking credits	$12 857
Total income	$42 857
Less deductions	$1 000
Taxable income	$41 857

Calculating tax payable/tax refund

Tax payable ($41 857 × 15%)	$6 278
Less dividend franking credits	$12 857
Net tax refund	$6 579

As the dividend franking credits exceed the tax payable your SMSF will get a $6579 tax refund. In contrast, if the same amount was returned in your individual tax return and your marginal rate of tax (plus Medicare levy) was 31.5 per cent (or higher), you would have been liable to pay tax on this amount.

Case study: receiving a superannuation pension

Albert is 60 years of age and has a $600 000 share portfolio paying 5 per cent dividends fully franked in his SMSF pension account. At the end of the financial year the pension account provided the following information:

Dividends	$30 000
Dividend franking credits	$12 857
Total amount credited	$42 857

As Albert is 60 years of age no tax is payable on the net earnings his super fund derived. He can withdraw a $42 857 tax-free pension which is excluded from his assessable income.

Tax tip

Explore the benefits you can gain from transferring shares that have decreased in value to your self managed superannuation fund. You will crystallise a capital loss that you can deduct from a capital gain, and you could qualify for a tax deduction if you're self-employed. Your super fund could sell the shares and invest the proceeds in other companies that have a capacity to appreciate in value.

Useful references

Australian Taxation Office publications

- *Division 7A—loans by private companies*
- *Income of individuals under the age of 18*
- *Listed investment company (LIC) dividends*
- *Non-assessable capital payments from a trust*
- *Setting up a self managed super fund* (NAT 71923)
- *Share of credits from a partnership*
- *Share of credits from a trust*
- *Special tax rules for under-18s*
- *Tax aspects of incorporating your business*

Australian Taxation Office interpretative decisions

- ID 2002/1070: *Income tax: trust with nil net income — refund of imputation credits*

- ID 2002/1071: *Income tax: trust with nil net income — refund of imputation credits*

- ID 2002/1100: *Income tax: franking tax offset — refund to trustee*

- ID 2004/859: *Income tax: family trust distribution tax — franking credits*

- ID 2005/31: *Income tax: streaming of franking credits — distribution to only one class of shareholder*

- ID 2006/158: *Income tax: the effect of indirectly receiving a franked distribution through trusts*

Other taxation rulings

- GSTD 2005/3: *Goods and services tax: are contracts for difference and financial spread betting contracts financial supplies?*

- TR 93/17: *Income tax: income tax deductions available to superannuation funds*

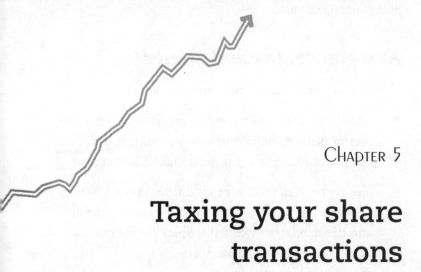

CHAPTER 5

Taxing your share transactions

There are umpteen tax rulings equivalent in size to a telephone book relating to the taxation of shares that you must comply with. Get them wrong and the Australian Taxation Office could come down on you like a tonne of bricks. It's good to know you can always consult a registered tax agent if you need assistance. In chapter 2 it was pointed out the way your share transactions are taxed is primarily dependent on whether you're classified as a share trader or a share investor. In this chapter I guide you through the key tax rules and regulations associated with owning shares that you'll need to be aware of.

At a glance: tax and shares

This is how your share transactions are taxed:

- *Dividends:* dividend payments are liable to tax when they're paid or credited to your account, and you can claim a franking credit if the dividend is franked.

- *Tax deductions:* certain expenditures you incur in deriving assessable income (such as trading profits and dividends) are tax deductible, but there must be a relevant nexus between the two to qualify as a tax deductible expense.

- *Trading profits and losses:* if you carry on a business as a share trader all your sales form part of your assessable income and all your purchases are tax deductible expenses. Your trading losses can be offset against other income you derive (for instance, salary and wages).

- *Capital gains and capital losses:* share investors are liable to pay capital gains tax if they make a capital gain on sale, but a capital loss can only be offset against a capital gain (see chapter 6).

- *Goods and services tax (GST):* no GST is payable in respect of share transactions, but you're liable to pay GST on your brokerage fees.

Dividends

Companies listed on the Australian Securities Exchange (ASX) normally declare and pay two dividends each year to their shareholders. They are an interim or mid-year dividend and a final or end-of-year dividend. Dividends are liable to tax when they're paid or credited to your account. Incidentally, you can request the company to remit your dividend payments directly to your nominated bank account.

Australia has adopted a dividend imputation system in respect of the payment of dividends to shareholders. Under this system, when a company declares a dividend it must inform its shareholders whether the dividend is franked or unfranked. If the dividend is franked you will receive a franking credit (or tax offset) that you can apply against the net tax payable (see following for more details). The relevant information is set out in the shareholder dividend statement you'll receive when a company pays you a dividend (see figure 5.1).

Figure 5.1: shareholder dividend statement

Shareholder Dividend Statement	
Fully Franked Final Dividend	
Year Ended 30 June 20XX	
Payment date	19 May 20XX
ABC Limited	
Class of shares	Ordinary shares
Dividend rate per share	$1.00
Number of shares held	10000
Franked amount	$10000
Franking credit	$4285
Dividend amount	$10000

You should record all your dividend payments on a spreadsheet in strict date order as set out in chapter 9, figure 9.1: summary of dividends received (p. 179). The payment of a franking credit is primarily dependent on whether a company has paid tax on its profits, and whether it has built up sufficient tax credits in its franking account. If the dividend is unfranked you won't get a franking credit. Incidentally, only resident Australian companies can pay you a franked dividend and only residents of Australia can claim a franking credit tax offset.

Tax tip

When you prepare your tax return for individuals you will need to insert your total dividend payments and franking credits at Item 12: Dividends, and more particularly at (S) Unfranked amount, (T) Franked amount and (U) Franking credit.

If the dividends you receive are substantial you may need to prepare an instalment activity statement and pay PAYG (pay-as-you-go) withholding tax on a monthly or quarterly basis. The Tax Office will inform you whether you'll need to do this. The tax you're liable to pay is credited against your end-of-financial-year assessment. For more information you can read ATO publication *PAYG instalments—how to complete your activity statement* (NAT 7392). You can get a copy from your local Tax Office or you can download a copy from its website <www.ato.gov.au>.

Tax trap

If you don't quote your tax file number to the company at the time you buy your shares, the company may withhold tax at the rate of 46.5 per cent from your dividend payment. This will normally happen if the dividend is unfranked. The amount withheld is applied against the tax payable, and you'll need to include the details in your tax return. Incidentally, when you prepare your tax return for individuals you'll need to insert the details at Item 12 (V): Tax file number amounts withheld from dividends.

Franking credits

As mentioned in the previous section, if a company pays you a franked dividend you will receive a franking credit. The size of the franking credit depends on the company tax rate (currently 30 per cent) and to what extent the dividend is franked. (At the time of writing, the Federal Labor Government has proposed to reduce the company tax rate to 29 per cent in the 2013–14 financial year and to 28 per cent in the 2014–15 financial year, which means the franking credit will reduce accordingly.) The following formula is used to calculate the franking credit.

Cash dividend $\times$ 30 $\div$ 70 = franking credit.

Incidentally, 30 $\div$ 70 is 'the company tax rate (0.30) $\div$ (1 − the company tax rate: 0.70)'. For instance, if a company pays you a $10 000 fully franked dividend you will receive $10 000 in cash plus a $4285 franking credit

($10 000 × 30 ÷ 70 = $4285; see figure 5.1). Conversely, if the dividend is franked to, for instance, 50 per cent, you will receive $10 000 in cash and the franking credit is reduced by 50 per cent from $4285 to $2142.

When you lodge your tax return for individuals you must include both the franked dividend (for instance, $10 000) and the franking credit (for instance, $4285) as part of your assessable income. You're liable to pay tax on the 'grossed-up amount' ($14 285) at your marginal rates of tax, and the franking credit ($4285) is applied against the net tax payable. If your franking credits exceed the net tax payable the Tax Office will refund the balance to you. This could significantly benefit low income earners. For instance, no tax is payable once your taxable income falls below $16 000 (per 2010–11 tax rates). Under these circumstances the entire franking credits will be refunded to you and the overall return on your investment will increase. For more details see Tax Office publication *Refund of franking credits*.

 Tax tip

If you don't need to lodge a tax return (for instance, you're a senior Australian aged 65 or more and you derive less than a statutory amount of taxable income), the Tax Office will refund any franking credits you received from your shares. To get this refund you'll need to get hold of Tax Office publication *Refund of franking credits instructions and application for individuals* (NAT 4105); you can get this publication from the Tax Office or you can download a copy from its website.

Tax trap

Ordinarily, to qualify for a franking credit you must hold your shares 'at risk' (meaning that they could fall in value) for a minimum qualifying period. This qualifying period is 45 days for ordinary shares and 90 days for preference shares. You could be denied a franking credit if you buy and sell your shares within the qualifying period and you receive a franked dividend from the company. However, under the 'small shareholder exemption provisions' this rule won't apply if the total franking credits you receive during the financial year is $5000 or less. This means you can effectively receive up to $11 666 franked dividends before the 45 days holding rule will apply ($11 666 × 30 ÷ 70 = $5000). For more details see Tax Office publication *Income from dividends*. You can download a copy from its website.

Case study: receiving a franked dividend

At the end of the financial year Anita received $15 000 interest and a $10 000 fully franked dividend from DEF Ltd. The franking credit was $4285 (see figure 5.1). When Anita lodges her tax return for individuals she'll need to include the $10 000 dividend plus the $4285 franking credit as part of her assessable income. She also incurred $785 expenditure in deriving her interest and dividends.

Tax return for individuals
Income

Interest	$15 000
Item 12: Dividends:	
Franked amount	$10 000
Franking credit	$4 285
Total income	$29 285
Less:	
Item D7: Interest and dividend deductions	$785
Taxable income	$28 500

Calculation of tax payable/refund

Tax payable on $28 500	$3 375
Plus:	
Medicare levy (1.5% × $28 500)	$427
Tax payable	$3 802
Less:	
Low income tax offset*	$1 500
Franking credits	$4 285
Total offsets	$5 785
Refund of tax	$1 983

*Anita is also entitled to a $1500 low income tax offset (per 2010–11 tax rates).

In this case study Anita will receive a $1983 refund of tax, being the balance of her unused franking credits. Incidentally, as a low income tax offset is not refundable, this amount is first applied against the tax payable and then the franking credit.

Tax trap

As part of the Tax Office's ongoing compliance program, it will regularly match dividends paid by Australian companies against individual tax returns. Penalties may apply if you fail to disclose the correct amount of dividends in your tax return. For more details see Tax Office publication *Sharemarket transactions data matching*.

Getting a tax lesson: how dividend franking works

If you're experiencing difficulty coming to terms with the dividend imputation system the following explanation may be of assistance. Getting a franked dividend is similar to receiving a net salary or wage from your employer. Your net pay is equivalent to your receiving a cash dividend payment, and the franking credit is equivalent to your employer withholding tax from your gross pay (as illustrated below). So let's assume you own all the shares in a company and that company makes a $10000 net profit. After it pays 30 per cent company tax on its profits, the net balance is distributed to its shareholders (in this case to you).

Company accounts

Net profit	$10000
Less:	
Tax payable (30%)	$3000
Net distributable profit	$7000

> **Company distribution to shareholders**
>
> | | |
> |---|---:|
> | Cash dividend (net pay) | $7 000 |
> | Franking credit (tax withheld) | $3 000 |
> | Gross dividend (gross pay) | $10 000 |
>
> When you lodge your tax return for individuals you're liable to pay tax on the grossed-up dividend amount of $10 000 (which is equivalent to your gross pay), and you can claim a franking credit in respect of the amount of tax that was withheld ($3000). It's as simple as that!

Dividend reinvestment plans

When a company declares a dividend it will normally pay you a cash amount. If a company has a dividend reinvestment plan you could elect to receive additional shares in lieu of the cash dividend payment. These shares are normally offered to you at a discount and no brokerage fees or GST is payable. Although you will receive additional shares in lieu of a cash payment, you must include the dividend as part of your assessable income. You will be deemed to have acquired the additional shares on the date the dividend is paid. The cost base of the shares you receive will equal the amount of the dividend that you used to buy the additional shares.

Case study: dividend reinvestment plan

Marina owns 1000 shares in ABC Ltd. On 15 November the company declared 35 cents per share dividend payable on 17 December. Under the company's dividend reinvestment plan Marina has elected to receive additional shares in lieu of the cash dividend payment of $350. Under the dividend reinvestment plan the market price of ABC Ltd shares (after allowing for a 5 per cent discount) was $13.46. On 17 December Marina received an additional 26 shares in lieu of the $350 dividend payment. When Marina lodges her tax return for individuals she will need to declare the $350 dividend as part of her assessable income. She will be deemed to have acquired the 26 shares on 17 December (the date the dividend was paid). The cost base of the 26 shares she purchased is $350 (26 × $13.46 per share).

 Tax tip

In ATO interpretative decision ID 2004/652 the Tax Office states moneys paid by a company to its shareholders as a capital return do not constitute a dividend.

Foreign dividends

If you receive a foreign dividend and withholding tax was withheld from the payment, you'll need to include both the dividend and amount of foreign tax withheld as part of your assessable income. You're liable to pay tax on the grossed-up amount, and you can claim a foreign tax credit in respect of the amount withheld from your dividend payment. This is to avoid double taxation.

If your foreign tax credit exceeds the net tax payable the excess cannot be refunded to you (as is the case if you receive a franking credit). For more details see Tax Office publication *Guide to foreign income tax offset rules* (NAT 72923).

Case study: receiving a foreign dividend

Roberta received a $1700 dividend from a UK-based company and 15 per cent withholding tax was withheld from the payment (namely, $300). When Roberta lodges her tax return for individuals she'll need to include $2000 as part of her assessable income ($1700 dividend plus the $300 tax withheld.). This amount is liable to tax at her marginal rates of tax and she can claim a $300 foreign tax credit in respect of the foreign tax withheld. Roberta will need to insert the relevant details at Item 20: Foreign source income and foreign assets or property, in her tax return for individuals (supplementary section).

Taxing your profits and losses

If you carry on a business as a share trader all your trading transactions are on *revenue account*. This means all your sales are included as part of your assessable income and all your purchases are tax deductible expenses (for more details see chapter 2). Further, any expenses necessarily incurred in carrying on a share trading business for the purposes of gaining or producing trading profits are tax deductible expenses (see next section for more details). In contrast, this is not the case if you are a share investor as share purchases and sales are on *capital account*. This means any capital gain a share investor derives and any capital loss incurred will fall for consideration under the CGT provisions (see chapter 6).

Claiming a tax deduction

Under Australian tax law, to qualify for a tax deduction there must be a relevant connection between the expenditure you incur and the derivation of your assessable income. The Income Tax Assessment Act points out that you can deduct from your assessable income any loss or outgoing to the extent:

- it is incurred in gaining or producing assessable income (for instance, dividends); or

- it is necessarily incurred in carrying on a business (for instance, share trading) for the purposes of gaining or producing assessable income (such as the profits you derive from share trading).

But you can't claim a loss or outgoing to the extent it is capital, private or domestic in nature.

What all this means is if you are a share investor you can only claim a tax deduction if there is a relevant connection between the expenditure you incur and the derivation of assessable income such as your dividend payments. Share traders, on the other hand, get two bites of the apple: they can also claim any loss or outgoing that is necessarily incurred in carrying on a business as a share trader that is not ordinarily available to share investors (see next section for more details). But you can't claim a tax deduction if it turns out to be capital, private or domestic in nature.

What is tax deductible?

The following list provides examples of the types of expenditure you can claim if you are a share investor or share trader:

- account-keeping fees in respect of accounts held for investment purposes

- borrowing expenses (for more details see chapter 7)

- costs of subscriptions to sharemarket information services and specialist investment journals (provided it's for the purposes of deriving assessable income)

- expenditure incurred in relation to the management of your share portfolio (for instance, telephone calls, bookkeeping and postage)

- depreciation (decline in value) of your computer to the extent it's related to managing your investments and more particularly your share portfolio

- interest on borrowings used for the purposes of deriving assessable income (for instance, to buy shares that pay dividends); there must be a reasonable expectation that you will derive a dividend from the shares you purchase (for more details see chapter 7)

- internet access in respect of managing your share portfolio and to buy and sell shares online

- ongoing management fees or retainers paid to investment advisers in respect of investment-related matters; but you can't claim a tax deduction in respect of a fee paid for drawing up an initial investment plan

- rental fee for a safe deposit box to safeguard your investment-related securities such as your share portfolio documents

- tax agent fees in respect of managing your tax affairs and lodgement of your individual tax return

- travel expenses to attend a company's annual general meeting or consult a stockbroker.

 Tax trap

If you are a share investor, a loss on sale of shares is not a tax deductible expense; but you will be considered to have incurred a capital loss. Further, you cannot claim brokerage fees and GST as tax deductible expenses, as the purchase of shares is capital in nature. But these costs can be taken into account when calculating a capital gain or capital loss (see chapter 6).

Share trader

If you carry on a business as a share trader you can claim the following additional tax deductions as they are considered to be necessarily incurred in carrying on a business:

- the purchase price of your shares; this is because the purchase of shares is regarded as the purchase of trading stock

- brokerage and GST you incur when you buy and sell shares

- costs of maintaining an office

- losses incurred in carrying on a business as a securities and commodities trader

- mobile phone call costs incurred in accessing live market share prices

- depreciation of share trading software

- interest on borrowings to buy shares and more particularly your trading stock

- contributions to a complying super fund.

 Tax tip

You could be eligible to claim a tax deduction if you donate shares in listed public companies valued at $5000 or less that you've owned for at least 12 months to a deductible gift recipient. For more details see Tax Office publication *Gifts of shares valued at $5000 or less*.

Less common share transactions and taxation issues

If you own shares in a number of companies you may find these companies could contact you in respect to the following important issues.

Share buyback offer

When a company has surplus funds it can either invest them to grow the business, or it can use them to buy back shares them had previously issued. Under corporations law, companies can buy their shares back on the Australian Securities Exchange (called an on-market buyback), or they can enter into a buyback scheme with their shareholders (called an off-market buyback). Under an off-market buyback offer arrangement, the buyback price will normally consist of a capital component and a franked dividend component. The relevant details (particularly the tax issues) will be set out in the buyback offer booklet the company will issue to its shareholders. Whether you should participate in an off-market buyback will depend on:

- the conditions of the buyback offer

- the cost base of your shares

- the market value of those shares as determined by an ATO formula set out in tax determination TD 2004/22. The Tax Office will ordinarily issue a class ruling in respect of the taxation treatment of specific company return of capital share buyback schemes. You can access these on the Tax Office website.

Case study: off-market buyback scheme

Three years ago Malcolm purchased a number of shares in Apex Ltd at $10 per share. The company has entered into an off-market buyback scheme with its shareholders. According to the buyback offer booklet the buyback price is $24 made up of a $12 capital component and a $12 dividend component (franking credit $5.14). For capital gains tax purposes the Tax Office has deemed the market value of the buyback price to be $14.50 (as determined by a formula set out in tax determination TD 2004/22). If Malcolm participates in the buyback offer and sells 1000 shares he will be taxed as follows:

⇒ He will make a $4500 capital gain on sale [Capital proceeds $14 500 (1000 × $14.50) – cost base $10 000 (1000 × $10) = $4500].

⇒ As the shares were owned for more than 12 months only 50 per cent of the capital gain is liable to tax.

⇒ The $12 000 dividend and $5140 franking credit component will be included as part of Malcolm's assessable income, and he can claim a $5140 franking credit tax offset.

Bonus shares

If a company issues bonus shares it means shareholders will receive additional shares free of charge. Under Australian tax law the paid-up value of bonus shares is ordinarily not assessed as a dividend (unless you have the option of being paid a cash dividend). Under the CGT provisions the taxation treatment of bonus shares depends on when you acquired your original shares. If you acquired your original shares before 20 September 1985, you will be deemed to have acquired your bonus shares before 20 September 1985, and no CGT is payable on disposal. Conversely, if you acquired your original shares on or after 20 September 1985, you will be deemed to have acquired your bonus shares on the date you acquired your original shares. Under these circumstances you will need to adjust the cost base of your original shares. When you do this calculation you will be effectively reducing the cost base of all the shares you own.

Case study: original shares acquired before 20 September 1985

Ramona acquired 1000 shares in DEF Ltd at $10 per share on 18 July 1984. Today DEF Ltd issued 100 bonus shares to its shareholders. Ramona will be deemed to have acquired her 100 bonus shares on 18 July 1984. As she acquired her original shares before 20 September 1985, the bonus shares are excluded from the CGT provisions and are not liable to CGT on disposal.

Case study: original shares acquired on or after 20 September 1985

Alexander acquired 1000 shares in ABC Ltd at $10 per share on 11 October 2010 (cost base $10 000). Today

ABC Ltd issued 100 bonus shares to its shareholders. Alexander will be deemed to have acquired his bonus shares on 11 October 2010. As Alexander acquired his original shares on or after 20 September 1985 he will need to adjust the cost base of his original shares as follows:

Original cost base ÷ (original shares + bonus shares)

$10000 ÷ (1000 + 100) = $9.09

According to the above calculations the cost base of Alexander's 1100 shares has been reduced to $9999 (which is equivalent to $9.09 per share (1100 × $9.09)). Incidentally, as you are effectively reducing the cost base of each share you are potentially liable to pay more CGT on disposal.

Scrip-for-scrip rollover

If you own shares in a company that has been taken over by another company, you may qualify for CGT relief if you exchange your shares for shares in the takeover company, and you make a capital gain as a result of the takeover. Incidentally, you could qualify for partial CGT relief if you receive shares plus a cash payment. The company will normally set out the various taxation issues you'll need to consider if you find yourself in this situation. For specific scrip-for-scrip rollover arrangements you can visit the ATO website (go to 'class rulings') or you can contact the company. The Tax Office has also issued a publication *Takeovers and mergers, scrip-for-scrip rollover*.

Demergers

If you own shares in a company that's restructuring (referred to as demergers), unless the company advises you otherwise, dividends paid under a demerger are not subject to tax. Further, you could qualify for CGT relief if you satisfy certain conditions and you may need to adjust the cost base and reduced cost base of your shares. For more details see Tax Office publication *Demergers: cost base rules tax determination*. The Tax Office has issued class rulings in respect of the taxation treatment of specific company demergers. It has also issued the following interpretative decisions.

- ID 2002/639: *Income tax: shares received as a result of a company split — treated as a dividend*

- ID 2003/914: *Capital gains tax: demergers — cost base allocation rules in the demerger provisions*

- ID 2003/916: *Income tax: capital gains tax: demerger — CGT discount*

You can obtain a copy of these class rulings and inter-pretative decisions from the ATO or you can visit its website.

Rights issues

Under a rights issue, when a company needs to raise additional capital it will give its shareholders the right to buy additional shares at a specified price from the company. There is no income tax liability at the time of issue. To encourage shareholders to participate, the shares are normally offered at a discount and no brokerage fees or GST is payable. Shareholders will be given a specific period of time to exercise their right to buy the shares (for instance, three weeks). If you do not exercise your right to buy the shares by the due date the offer will lapse. The number of shares you can buy is normally limited to either a certain dollar amount (for instance, you can buy up to a maximum of $10 000) or to the number of shares you currently hold. For example, you own 10 000 shares and the company offers a one-for-10 rights issue (meaning you can buy one additional share for every 10 you own); in this case you can buy up to 1000 shares.

The company may offer a 'non-renounceable rights issue' or a 'renounceable rights issue'. A non-renounceable rights issue means only shareholders can buy the shares at the specified price by the due date. If you do not exercise your right to buy the shares by the due date the offer will lapse and there are no tax consequences. A renounceable rights issue, on the other hand, means shareholders can either exercise their right to buy the shares, or they can sell their rights on the ASX. The person who buys the rights from you can exercise their right to purchase the shares at the specified price.

Case study: non-renounceable rights issue

Andrew is a share investor who owns 10 000 shares in DEF Ltd. He originally paid $3 per share for them on 14 January. On 19 April the company announced a one-for-10 non-renounceable rights issue at $4.60 per share. The offer will close on 18 May and the market price is currently $5.80. This means Andrew has the right to buy 1000 shares from the company before the expiry date. If Andrew exercises his right to buy them, the cost base of these shares will be $4600 (1000 × $4.60). Under the CGT provisions Andrew will be considered to own two separate CGT assets with different cost bases and purchase dates, namely:

⇒ 10000 shares @ $3 per share ($30000) purchased on 14 January.

⇒ 1000 shares @ $4.60 per share ($4600) purchased on 18 May.

If Andrew decides not to exercise his right to buy them, the rights issue will lapse on 18 May and there are no tax consequences. On the other hand, if Andrew exercises his right to buy them, he will pay $4.60 for a share that is currently trading at $5.80, and he will derive an unrealised capital gain that is not liable to tax until the shares are sold.

Case study: renounceable rights issue

In the previous case study, if the rights issue is a renounceable rights issue Andrew can sell the rights on the ASX. The amount he will receive will ordinarily be around $1200 (being the difference between $5.80 (current market price) and $4.60 (issue price) × 1000) less brokerage fees and GST. Andrew will be considered to have made a $1200 capital gain that's liable to tax. Incidentally, the person who buys the right to purchase the shares at the fixed price of $4.60 (or $5.80 when the $1200 is taken into account) will be ahead if the shares continue to increase in value before the rights expire (for instance, to $6.80 on the expiry date).

Employee share schemes

If you acquire qualifying shares or options under an employee share scheme that's below the current market price, you could be liable to pay tax on the discount you receive in the financial year you acquire the shares or options. The discount is the difference between the market price of the shares or options and the acquisition price. You will need to include the value of the discount at Item 24: Other income, in your tax return for individuals (supplementary section). If you elect to be taxed 'upfront' you could qualify for a $1000 upfront tax concession where the first $1000 of the discount is exempt from tax. This is on the condition that your adjusted taxable income is less than $180 000. However, you can elect under the deferral option to defer the payment of tax until a later date (the maximum deferral period is seven years), provided certain conditions are met and there's a real risk of forfeiture of the shares during the deferral period. It's also possible for you to defer the payment of tax to acquire shares worth up to $5000 per annum under a salary sacrifice arrangement. For more details you can read Tax Office publication *Employee share schemes—information for employees.* You can download a copy from its website.

Shares from a deceased estate

The taxation treatment of shares from a deceased estate depends on when the deceased originally acquired them. Under the CGT provisions:

- If the deceased acquired the shares before 20 September 1985, the beneficiary will be deemed to have acquired them from the deceased on the date of death at their market value.

- If the deceased acquired the shares on or after 20 September 1985, the beneficiary will be deemed to have acquired the shares on the date of death at the value the deceased originally acquired them (namely the deceased's cost base). This means the beneficiary is liable to pay CGT on any increase in value during the time the deceased owned the shares, plus any further increase in value during the time the beneficiary owned them.

Case study: inheriting pre-20 September 1985 shares

On 18 March 1983 Debra purchased 10 000 shares in XYZ Ltd (total cost $20 000). Debra died today and bequeathed the shares to her daughter Lisa. The market value of these shares on the date of death was $50000. Lisa will be deemed to have acquired the 10000 shares in XYZ Ltd on the date of death at their market value (namely $50000), and this value will become the cost base. If Lisa sells the shares one year later and receives $60000 for them she will make a $10000 capital gain (capital proceeds $60000 less cost base $50000). As the shares were owned overall for more than 12 months only 50 per cent of the capital gain is liable to tax. Conversely, if the shares were sold for $40000 Lisa will incur a $10000 capital loss.

Case study: inheriting post-20 September 1985 shares

On 13 April 2009 Harbhajan purchased 5000 shares in ABC Ltd (cost base $25000). Harbhajan died today and bequeathed the shares to his son Kapil. The market value of these shares on the date of death was $90000. As the deceased acquired the shares on or after 20 September 1985, Kapil is deemed to have acquired the shares on the date of death at the value the deceased originally acquired them (namely $25000), and this value will become the cost base. In this case the market value is ignored. If Kapil sells the shares and receives $100000 for them, he will make a $75000 capital gain (capital proceeds $100000 less cost base $25000). As the shares were owned overall for more than 12 months only 50 per cent capital gain is liable to tax.

Tax trap

If a deceased had accumulated capital losses at the date of death, these losses can't be transferred to the beneficiaries. From a tax-planning point of view you should weigh up the benefits of selling your profitable companies and taking a capital gain whenever you have accumulated capital losses on hand.

Tax tip

Following are a few things to keep in mind when it comes to the taxation of shares:

⇒ Explore the benefit of buying shares in the name of adult family members (for instance, a spouse or adult child) who pay no tax or have a low marginal rate of tax (for instance, 15 per cent). This is particularly worth considering if their taxable income is below $16 000 as no tax is payable on this amount (per 2010–11 tax rates).

⇒ If you made a capital gain at the beginning of the financial year, you can delay the payment of tax until the next financial year.

⇒ Capital gains can be applied against revenue losses.

How to complete your tax return

In chapter 1 it was pointed out that residents of Australia are required to lodge an annual tax return for individuals disclosing the taxable income they derive from all sources whether in or out of Australia. Taxable income equals *assessable income less allowable deductions*. The following case study shows you how to calculate your taxable income and tax payable.

Case study: how to complete your tax return

At the end of the financial year Toula, who is a resident of Australia, derived the following *assessable income*:

⇒ $50 000 salary (the pay-as-you-go-withholding tax was $9300)

⇒ $4000 capital gain on sale of shares she held for more than 12 months

⇒ $10 000 franked dividend (the franking credit was $4285)

⇒ $1700 dividend from a UK-based company ($300 withholding tax had been deducted).

Toula's *allowable deductions* were $3285 interest on borrowings to buy shares in companies that pay dividends.

Toula is liable to pay tax on the assessable income she derived from all sources whether in or out of Australia. This means she'll need to include both the $1700 foreign dividend she received from the UK plus $300 withholding tax as part of her assessable income (namely, $2000 total). She will also need to include both the franked dividend and franking credit as well. With respect to the $4000 capital gain on sale, as the shares were held for more than 12 months, only 50 per cent of the capital gain (namely, $2000) is liable to tax. The balance is exempt and excluded from her assessable income. Toula can claim the following tax offsets:

⇒ $300 withholding tax she paid in the UK

⇒ $4285 dividend franking credit.

Tax return for individuals
Assessable income

Salary or wages	$50 000
Dividends:	
Franked amount	$10 000
Franking credit	$4 285
Foreign dividend	$1 700
Withholding tax	$300
Capital gain	$2 000
Total assessable income	$68 285
Less allowable deductions:	
Interest and dividend expenses	$3 285
Taxable income	$65 000

Tax payable/tax refund

Tax payable on $65 000	$13 050

Case study (cont'd)

Plus:

Medicare levy (1.5% × $65 000)	$975
Tax payable	$14 025

Less:

Tax withheld on salary	$9 300
Credit for withholding tax	$300
Franking credit	$4 285
Total tax offsets and other credits	$13 885
Tax payable	$140

In this case Toula is liable to pay $140 in tax.

Useful references

Australian Taxation Office publications

- *Bonus shares*

- *Demergers: overview*

- *Dividend reinvestment plans*

- *How to claim a foreign tax credit* (NAT 2338)

- *Imputation essentials*

- *Interest and dividend deductions*

- *Managing the tax affairs of someone who has died*

- *Reporting withholding and investment income payments* (NAT 15073)

- *Retail premiums paid to shareholders where share entitlements not taken up or not available*

- *Rights issues: taxation treatment of call options*

- *Share buy-backs*

- *You and your shares: rights issue*

Australian Taxation Office interpretative decisions

- ID 2002/690: *Income tax: refund of excess franking tax offset—franked dividends paid on or after 1 July 2000*

- ID 2002/831: *Income tax: deductibility of mobile phone call costs for a share trader to access live market information*

- ID 2002/844: *Income tax: deductibility of brokerage fees and stamp duty for a share trader*

- ID 2002/948: *Income tax: travel expenses—to attend company AGM*

- ID 2002/1066: *Income tax: share investor—deductibility of share brokerage costs*

- ID 2004/652: *Income tax: return of capital: not a dividend*

- ID 2006/243: *Income tax: assessability of dividends paid in respect of an underlying share that is the subject of an endowment warrant*

- ID 2010/21: *Income tax: frankable distributions and non-share dividends*

- ID 2010/52: *Deductions and expenses: short sale transactions and securities lending arrangements*

Other taxation rulings

- TD 2004/1: *Income tax: are the costs of subscriptions to sharemarket information services and investment journals deductible under section 8-1 of the* Income Tax Assessment Act 1997?

CHAPTER 6

Taxing your capital gains and losses

If you are a share investor, any capital gain you make or capital loss you incur on sale of your shares will fall for consideration under the capital gains tax (CGT) provisions. These provisions were first introduced on 19 September 1985, and apply to CGT assets that you acquire after this date. So if you're still holding shares you bought before 20 September 1985, any capital gain or capital loss you make on sale is disregarded and excluded from your assessable income. This is great news if the shares are continually appreciating in value, but bad news if the current market price is below the purchase price, as you'll miss out on claiming a capital loss. In this chapter I examine the impact of the CGT provisions on your shareholdings and explain how you are taxed.

How a capital gain is calculated

A liability to pay CGT arises when there is a CGT event. This will normally happen when you sell your shares or gift them to someone. The following formula is used to calculate a capital gain.

Capital proceeds – cost base = capital gain.

The 'capital proceeds' is the amount you receive on sale, which is normally a cash payment. It can also include the market value of property or a combination of both. The 'cost base' with respect to shares is ordinarily the purchase price plus incidental costs associated with buying and selling them, such as brokerage fees and GST. It may also include 'non-capital costs' such as non-deductible interest on a loan (see section Non-capital Costs). For more details you can read Tax Office publication *What is the cost base?* The following example (with values I've inserted) illustrates how a capital gain is calculated:

Capital proceeds (sale price)		$10 000
Less:		
Cost base:		
Purchase price	$6 000	
Incidental costs of purchase (brokerage fees and GST)	$100	
Incidental costs of sale (brokerage fees and GST)	$110	$6 210
Capital gain		$3 790

Under the CGT provisions a sale (CGT event) will ordinarily arise at the time of the making of the contract. This means you'll be considered to have bought or sold your shares on the date your stockbroker buys or sells them on your behalf rather than on the settlement date. If you make a capital gain the amount of tax you're liable to pay depends on whether you bought the shares before or after 21 September 1999. This was the date when the federal government changed the rules for calculating a capital gain on sale of CGT assets.

Shares bought after 21 September 1999

There are two basic rules associated with calculating a capital gain in respect of shares you acquire on or after 21 September 1999. They are relatively straightforward and easy to follow:

- If you sell shares within 12 months of buying them and you make a capital gain, the entire amount is liable to tax at your marginal rates of tax (which can vary between 0 per cent and 45 per cent). This gain is called a 'non-discount capital gain', meaning the entire amount is taxable, and is included as part of assessable income you derive from various sources (see figure 6.1, overleaf).

- If you sell shares you've owned for more than 12 months and you make a capital gain, only half the gain is liable to tax at your marginal rates of tax. The balance is exempt and excluded from assessable income. This gain is called a 'discount capital gain', meaning you can reduce the capital gain by 50 per cent. So there is an incentive for you to keep shares that are appreciating in value for at least 12 months. The amount that's taxable is included as part of the assessable income you derive from various sources (see figure 6.1).

If you make a capital loss (for instance, on another parcel of shares) or you have prior year capital losses you have not yet claimed, you can deduct the capital loss from the capital gain you made.

 Tax tip

A capital loss on sale of shares can be deducted from a capital gain you made on sale of another CGT asset (for instance, real estate).

Case study: calculating a capital gain

Two years ago Samuel bought 1000 shares in Brambles Ltd at $6 per share and paid $100 purchase costs. According to the buy contract note he received from his stockbroker the total cost was $6100. Today Samuel contacted his stockbroker and sold his 1000 shares in Brambles Ltd at $10 per share and paid $150 sale costs. According to the sell contract note the net proceeds on sale was $9850 ($10 000 – $150).

Figure 6.1: capital gains tax

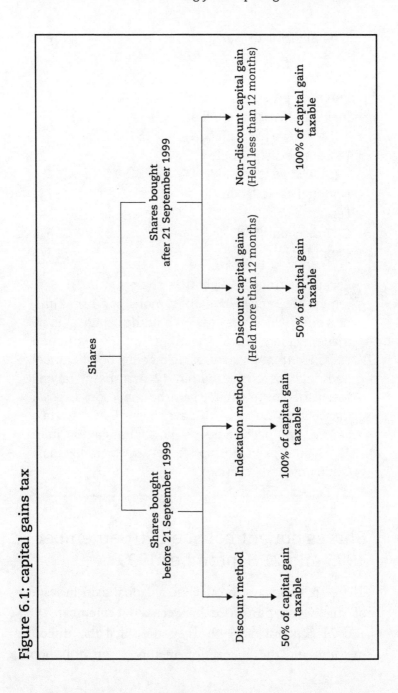

Capital proceeds (sale price)		$10 000
Less:		
Cost base:		
Purchase price	$6 000	
Incidental costs of purchase (brokerage fees and GST)	$100	
Incidental costs of sale (brokerage fees and GST)	$150	$6 250
Notional capital gain		$3 750
Less:		
CGT discount (50%)		$1 875
Capital gain		$1 875

Because Samuel bought the shares after 21 September 1999 and held them for more than 12 months, he's only liable to pay tax on half the capital gain he made, namely $1875. The other half is exempt and excluded from his assessable income. But if Samuel had sold his shares within 12 months of buying them the entire capital gain he made on disposal (namely $3750) would have been liable to tax. Samuel will need to insert the capital gain at Item 18: Capital gains, in his tax return for individuals (supplementary section).

Shares bought between 20 September 1985 and 21 September 1999

There are two ways to calculate a capital gain in respect of shares you purchased between 20 September 1985 and 21 September 1999. They are called the 'discount method' and the 'indexation method'. You can choose either method to calculate the amount that is taxable. The method you'll choose is the one that will give you the best result (namely, paying the least amount of tax).

Ordinarily you'll find the discount method is the preferred option as only 50 per cent of the capital gain is taxable (as is the case today if you keep your shares for more than 12 months). Under the indexation method it can get a little tricky, as you'll need to reduce any part of the capital gain that arises due to inflation. This was how it was done before they changed the rules on 21 September 1999. A major drawback with the indexation method is you can only adjust for inflation between the dates you bought the shares up until 30 September 1999. As many years have now passed since the new rules were introduced, the indexation method has become somewhat redundant and is of academic interest only.

Discount method

If you use the discount method only 50 per cent of the capital gain is taxable, as is the case with shares you buy after 21 September 1999 and keep for more than 12 months. The balance is exempt and excluded from assessable income (see figure 6.1).

Case study: using the discount method

On 16 October 1994 Sergio purchased 1000 shares in Merchant Bank Ltd. According to the buy contact note he paid $15 000 and incurred $150 brokerage fees and GST to buy them. Sergio sold the shares today. According to the sell contract note the sale price was $27 000 and he paid $200 brokerage fees and GST to sell them. If Sergio elects to use the discount method, only 50 per cent of the capital gain is liable to tax; the balance is exempt and excluded from his assessable income. Under this method the capital gain is calculated as follows:

Capital proceeds (sale price)		$27 000
Less:		
Cost base:		
Purchase price	$15 000	
Incidental costs of purchase (brokerage fees and GST)	$150	
Incidental costs of sale (brokerage fees and GST)	$200	$15 350
Notional capital gain		$11 650
Less:		
CGT discount (50%)		$5 825
Capital gain		$5 825

Under the discount method Sergio is liable to pay tax on half the capital gain he made on disposal, namely $5825. Sergio will need to compare this result against the indexation method to find out which method will give him the better result (namely, paying the least amount of tax).

Indexation method

Before 21 September 1999, when you calculated a capital gain for tax purposes you were allowed to adjust the various elements of the cost base of your shares for inflation. As mentioned previously this was done to avoid paying tax on any gain that may have arisen due to inflation. The consumer price index (CPI) is used to make this adjustment. This is the index Australia uses to measure its rate of inflation (see table 6.1, overleaf). In the previous case study, if Sergio were to use the indexation method, he would need to adjust each element of the cost base of his shares for inflation (namely the $15 000 purchase price plus $150 purchase costs) between the date he bought the shares (16 October 1994) and 30 September 1999. The appropriate CPI figures to do this adjustment are taken from table 6.1. As Sergio bought the shares on 16 October 1994 he will use the CPI figure for the quarter ending 31 December 1994 (namely 112.8), while the CPI figure for 30 September 1999 was 123.4. The following formula is used to make this adjustment.

CPI at 30 September 1999 (123.4) ÷ CPI at date of purchase (112.8) = 1.093.

Capital proceeds (sale price)		$27 000
Less:		
Indexed cost base:		
Purchase price ($15 000 × 1.093)	$16 395	
Incidental costs of purchase ($150 × 1.093)	$164	
Incidental costs of sale	$200	$16 759
Capital gain		$10 241

Table 6.1: Consumer Price Index

Year	31 Mar.	30 June	30 Sept.	31 Dec.
1985	0	0	71.3	72.7
1986	74.4	75.6	77.6	79.8
1987	81.4	82.6	84.0	85.5
1988	87.0	88.5	90.2	92.0
1989	92.9	95.2	97.4	99.2
1990	100.9	102.5	103.3	106.0
1991	105.8	106.0	106.6	107.6
1992	107.6	107.3	107.4	107.9
1993	108.9	109.3	109.8	110.0
1994	110.4	111.2	111.9	**112.8**
1995	114.7	116.2	117.6	118.5
1996	119.0	119.8	120.1	120.3
1997	120.5	120.2	119.7	120.0
1998	120.3	121.0	121.3	121.9
1999	121.8	122.3	**123.4**	

Source: Australian Bureau of Statistics

Incidentally, as Sergio incurred his incidental costs of sale after 30 September 1999, he cannot adjust the $200 he incurred for inflation.

If Sergio elects to use the indexation method the capital gain that's liable to tax is $10 241. In this case Sergio will choose the discount method as he's only liable to pay tax on $5825 rather than $10 241 under the indexation method. So that's why the indexation method is basically of academic interest only!

Tax trap

If you make a capital loss on sale of any shares you purchased before 30 September 1999 you can't index your cost base for inflation.

 Tax tip

In the event of a return of capital to shareholders you will need to reduce the cost base and reduced cost base of the shares you own. If the return of capital is more than the cost base, the difference is treated as a capital gain. For instance, if the return of capital is $1 and the cost base of your shares is $0.80 you will derive a $0.20 capital gain. Incidentally, a return of capital cannot create a capital loss. The Tax Office will ordinarily issue class rulings in respect of the taxation treatment of return of capital proposals of specific companies. You can access them on the Tax Office website <www.ato.gov.au>.

Unrealised capital gains

A major benefit of being classified as a share investor is your unrealised capital gains are not liable to tax until the shares are sold. And if you hold them for more than 12 months, only half the capital gain is taxable. So it's possible for you to pick and choose the best time to take some profit off the table.

For instance:

- wait until you make a capital loss, as you can deduct the capital loss from the capital gain

- wait until your taxable income falls below a particular marginal rate of tax threshold (for instance, if your taxable income falls below $37 000 (per 2010–11 tax rates), your marginal rate of tax will fall from 30 per cent to 15 per cent)

- wait until your taxable income falls below $16 000 (per 2010–11 tax rates), as no tax is payable

- wait until beginning of the financial year, as no tax is payable until you receive your 'notice of assessment' in the following financial year.

Case study: unrealised capital gain

Three years ago Tony purchased 1000 shares in ABC Ltd and paid $1 per share for them (total outlay $1000). Their current market price is $6.50 per share ($6500). Over a three-year period Tony has accumulated an unrealised capital gain amounting to $5500. So until he sells the shares and crystallises a capital gain no tax is payable. Tony can pick the right moment to take a profit.

 Tax tip

If you intend to sell your shares and take a capital gain, explore the tax benefits you could gain from selling part of your share holdings at the end of one financial year, and the balance at the beginning of the next financial year. If you do this you will be able to spread the capital gain over two financial years. This could benefit investors whose taxable income is less than $16000 as no tax is payable if you earn less than this amount.

Capital loss

If you're a share investor and you incur a capital loss, you cannot deduct the capital loss from assessable income you derive from other sources. Under the CGT provisions a capital loss can only be offset against a capital gain. If you make no capital gains in the same financial year you incur a capital loss, you can deduct the capital loss from any capital gains you may make in the future. Incidentally, when you calculate a capital loss you will use the 'reduced cost base' rather than the 'cost base'. Apart from a minor technical adjustment that mainly affects property transactions, the two terms are identical. The following formula is used to calculate a capital loss.

Capital proceeds − reduced cost base = capital loss.

The following case study shows you how to calculate a capital loss.

Case study: capital loss

Two years ago Olivia bought 1000 DEF Ltd shares at $9 per share and paid $150 purchase costs. According to the buy contract note she received from her stockbroker the total cost was $9150. Today Olivia contacted her stockbroker and sold her 1000 DEF Ltd shares at $4 per share and paid $100 sale costs. According to the sell contract note the net proceeds on sale was $3900.

Capital proceeds (sale price) (1000 × $4)		$4000
Less:		
Reduced cost base:		
Purchase price (1000 × $9)	$9000	
Incidental costs of purchase (brokerage fees and GST)	$150	
Incidental costs of sale (brokerage fees and GST)	$100	$9250
Capital loss		$5250

Olivia will need to insert the capital loss she made at Item 18: Capital gains, in her tax return for individuals (supplementary section) and more particularly at (V): Net capital losses carried forward to later income years (as she is not deducting the capital loss from a capital gain in this financial year).

 Tax tip

If you have unapplied capital losses from earlier years, the capital gain is offset against the earlier years in the order you incur your capital losses. For instance, if you incurred a capital loss three years ago and a further capital loss one year ago, the capital gain must first be applied against the capital loss you incurred three years ago, and then against the capital loss you incurred one year ago.

Claiming a capital loss

It can get a little tricky if you made a 'non-discount capital gain' and a 'discount capital gain' in the same financial year you incur a capital loss (or you have prior year capital losses not yet claimed). If you find yourself in this situation you should deduct the capital loss (and/or prior year capital losses) from your non-discount capital gains first. This is because you can claim a 50 per cent CGT discount only *after* you deduct all your current and prior year capital losses. So to get the full benefit of your capital losses you should deduct them from your non-discount gains first (as these don't qualify for the 50 per cent CGT discount). As there are no rules regarding the order in which you should claim a capital loss, the Tax Office leaves it up to you to make that decision. The following case study shows you what to do if you make a discount capital gain, a non-discount capital gain and a capital loss in the same financial year.

Case study: claiming a capital loss

During the financial year Patrick sold the following shares:

⇨ A parcel of DEF Ltd shares he owned for more than 12 months. The capital gain he made on sale was $30 000. This is a discount capital gain (meaning only 50 per cent of the amount is taxable).

⇨ A parcel of ABC Ltd shares he sold within 12 months of buying them. The capital gain on sale was $21 000. This is a non-discount capital gain (meaning the entire amount is taxable).

⇒ A parcel of XYZ Ltd shares. The capital loss he made on sale was $30 000.

To calculate the correct amount of the capital gain that's liable to tax Patrick will need to separate the non-discount capital gain ($21 000) and the discount capital gain ($30 000). In respect to the $30 000 capital loss he incurred, he will need to deduct the capital loss from the $21 000 non-discount capital gain first. This is because this gain doesn't qualify for the 50 per cent CGT discount. Any capital losses not yet claimed (in this case $9000) are deducted from the $30 000 discount capital gain. As Patrick is left with a net $21 000 discount capital gain, only 50 per cent of this amount (namely $10 500) is taxable. The balance is exempt and excluded from assessable income.

	Non-discount capital gain	Discount capital gain
ABC Ltd	$21 000	
DEF Ltd		$30 000
Less:		
Capital loss ($30 000)	$21 000	$9 000
Balance of capital gain	Nil	$21 000
Less:		
50% CGT discount		$10 500
Net capital gain	Nil	$10 500

But if Patrick had deducted the $30 000 capital loss from the $30 000 discount capital gain first, he would have been left with a $21 000 non-discount capital gain. This means he would have been liable to pay tax on $21000 rather than $10500 if the $30000 capital loss was first applied against the discount capital gain.

 Tax tip

Under the CGT provisions, if you own worthless shares in a company placed in liquidation, and the liquidator declares in writing that there is no likelihood that you will receive a distribution, you will be able to claim a capital loss. For more information see Tax Office publication *Shares and other securities that become worthless*. See also the dedicated website that deals with delisted companies <www.delisted.com.au>.

A capital loss has value

Under Australian tax law, if you're holding shares that have fallen in value you cannot claim an unrealised capital loss until the shares are actually sold. This could become a major dilemma if you've made a capital gain that's liable to tax (for instance $20000), and you're holding shares in a company that has fallen $20000 in value. If you don't want to pay tax on the capital gain you made, one option you could explore is to sell your loss companies and crystallise a capital loss. Although no one likes losing money, you should always keep in mind that a capital loss has value (and you will get out of a company that's losing you money!). This is because when the capital loss is offset against a capital gain, you will reduce the amount of tax payable on the capital gain you made. As mentioned in the previous section, when a capital loss is applied against a non-discount capital gain, you will get a 'full tax benefit' from utilising your capital loss. In the meantime, you will free up funds to buy shares in other companies that may give you a better chance of recouping the capital loss you incurred.

Case study: a capital loss has value

Three years ago Norma paid $30000 for a parcel of shares in NAB. These shares are currently worth $18000. Today Norma sold a parcel of shares in BHP Billiton and made a $12000 non-discount capital gain. Her marginal rate of tax (plus Medicare levy) is 31.5 per cent. The tax she's liable to pay on the $12000 capital gain is $3780 ($12000 × 31.5%). If she sells her NAB shares she will crystallise a $12000 capital loss. When the loss is deducted from the gain, she'll save $3780 in tax. In the meantime she can invest the money from the sale of her NAB shares in other companies that could increase in value.

 Tax trap

If you enter into an agreement to sell your shares, and you are to be paid by instalments over a number of years, you can't delay declaring a capital gain or capital loss until you receive the final payment. Under these circumstances a capital gain or capital loss will arise on the day you accept the offer to purchase your shares. For more details see Tax Office publication *Selling your shares and being paid by instalments*.

Wash sale arrangements

If you make a capital loss on sale of your shares and you buy them back immediately, there is a risk the Tax Office may disallow your capital loss. This is especially so if you had also made a capital gain in the same financial year that's liable to tax. If you sell shares predominantly to make a capital loss and you buy them back immediately, the Tax Office may take the view that the sale was predominantly done to gain a tax benefit. This is because you will still own the shares that created a capital loss, and you will gain a tax benefit when the capital loss is offset against a capital gain. This is commonly known as wash sale arrangements. In the previous case study, if Norma sold her NAB shares and bought them back immediately, she will still own the shares that created a capital loss, and she will gain a tax benefit ($3780 tax saving) when the $12000 capital loss is deducted from the $12000 capital gain. However, Norma can still buy shares in NAB at a later date. For instance, one month after she sold them she decided to reinvest in NAB again as the company's results had since improved. If you need more details, the Tax Office has issued taxpayer alert TA 2008/7 setting out the Tax Office's policy in respect of wash sale arrangements.

Identifying individual shares within a holding of identical shares

If you're accumulating shares in the same company over a period of time, you'll need to keep an accurate record of the different parcels you buy on different dates. This is because under the CGT provisions, each time you buy a parcel of identical shares the transaction is treated as a separate CGT asset with its own cost base and purchase date. Problems can arise if you sell individual shares within a holding of identical shares at a later date, as you'll need to know whether you had made a capital gain or capital loss. The buy and sell contract notes you receive from a stockbroker can help you solve this problem. The great thing about these documents is you can use the contract numbers to keep track of the shares you're buying and selling (see chapter 3). Where unidentifiable shares have been disposed of, the Tax Office will accept 'first in, first out' as a reasonable basis of identification. For more details see taxation determination TD 33: *Capital gains: how do you identify individual shares within a holding of identical shares?*

Case study: identifying individual shares

Over the past two years Boris has purchased three different parcels of 1000 shares in CBA on different dates. Under the CGT provisions Boris is considered to own three separate CGT assets with their own respective cost bases and purchase dates. He has kept all his buy contract notes to help him identify the shares he purchased on each occasion. The three buy contract notes recorded the following details:

⇒   1000 CBA shares purchased two years ago; total cost $40 000.

⇒   1000 CBA shares purchased one year ago; total cost $50 000.

⇒   1000 CBA shares purchased six months ago; total cost $60 000.

Today Boris contacted his stockbroker and sold 1000 shares in CBA. The sale price was $50 000. As Boris sold individual shares within a holding of identical shares, he will need to know which parcel of 1000 CBA shares he sold for the purposes of calculating whether he made a capital gain or capital loss. So which shares did Boris sell for the purposes of the Tax Act? In this case the decision will determine whether he had made a capital gain, capital loss or come out square. Technically speaking Boris will need to choose which parcel he intends to sell at the time of sale.

⇒   If he sells the 1000 CBA shares he bought two years ago he will make a $10 000 discount capital gain (which means only 50 per cent of the gain is taxable).

⇒   If he sells the 1000 CBA shares he bought one year ago he will come out square.

⇒   If he sells the 1000 CBA shares he bought six months ago he will make a $10 000 capital loss.

The parcel of CBA shares Boris will sell will depend on his personal circumstances, whether to crystallise a capital gain or capital loss or come out square. As Boris has kept his three buy contract notes he can identify the individual shares within a holding of identical shares. Incidentally, he can sell, say, 500 shares he bought two years ago and 500 shares he purchased six months ago and come out square that way by merely keeping track of the contract numbers of each buy contract note he holds.

 Tax tip

Where CGT assets such as shares are transferred to you as a consequence of a marriage breakdown you could qualify for CGT marriage breakdown rollover relief if you satisfy certain conditions. This means any capital gain or capital loss that would ordinarily arise at the time of transfer between spouses is disregarded. But you're liable to pay CGT when there is a subsequent disposal (for instance, when you sell the shares). For more details see Tax Office publication *Marriage breakdown and transferring of assets*.

Non-capital costs

Under the capital gains tax provisions, if you incur non-capital costs and more particularly interest on borrowings that are not a tax deductible expense, the amount can be included in the share's cost base. For instance, this could arise if you buy shares in companies that don't pay dividends or if you take out a capital protection loan (see chapter 7). But there is one condition: non-capital costs can be taken into account only if you make a capital gain, which means they can't be used to create or increase a capital loss. Further, this concession is available only for shares you purchase after 20 August 1991. The following case study shows you how this works.

Case study: non-capital costs: shares

Two years ago Keith borrowed money to buy a parcel of shares in a company that had never declared a dividend. The purchase price was $35 000 and he incurred $100 brokerage fees and GST. As there is no reasonable expectation that Keith will receive a dividend, the interest payments are not tax deductible. Because the shares were purchased after 20 August 1991 the interest payments can be included in the cost base. Keith sold the shares today for $50 000 and incurred $200 brokerage fees and GST. The accumulated non-deductible interest he incurred during the time he owned the shares amounted to $7000. The capital gain Keith made on disposal is calculated as follows:

Capital proceeds (sale price)		$50 000
Less:		
Cost base:		
Purchase price	$35 000	
Incidental costs (brokerage fees and GST)	$300	
Non-capital costs (interest)	$7 000	$42 300
Net capital gain		$7 700

However, if the sale price was $20000, Keith cannot take the $7000 non-capital costs (interest) into account, as they cannot be used to create or increase a capital loss. And if the sale price was, say, $38000, Keith can take only $2700 of his non-capital costs (interest) into account ($38000 – $35300 = $2700).

 Tax tip

In the event of a company announcing a share split you will need to adjust the cost base of each share you own. For example, one year ago you purchased 1000 shares for $20 per share (cost base $20000). Today the company announced a 2-for-1 share split. There are no tax consequences at the time of the share split. As you now own 2000 shares rather than 1000, the cost base of each share is reduced from $20 to $10 ($20000 ÷ 2000 = $10).

Useful references

Australian Taxation Office publications

- *Calculating a capital loss*
- *Capital gains tax: scrip for scrip roll-over — questions and answers*
- *Convertible notes (notes converted into shares)*
- *Guide to capital gains tax* (N4151)

- *Have you sold or given away any shares?*

- *Identifying when shares or units were acquired*

- *Marriage breakdown and capital gains tax—
  an overview*

- *Shares in a company in liquidation or administration*

- *Stapled securities and capital gains tax*

- *Takeovers and mergers, scrip-for-scrip rollover*

- *Worthless shares and financial instruments relating
  to company*

Australian Taxation Office interpretative decisions

- ID 2002/1095: *Income tax: capital gains tax:
  incidental costs forming part of the cost base*

CHAPTER 7

Tax-effective borrowing to buy shares

In this chapter I examine the main ways you can borrow money to buy shares, and discuss the tax issues you'll need to consider to comply with the Income Tax Assessment Act.

Under Australian tax law, interest on borrowings is a tax deductible expense to the extent it is incurred in gaining or producing assessable income or in carrying on a business for that purpose. So if you're a share trader the borrowed funds must be used for the purposes of deriving your trading profits and dividends. Conversely, if you're a share investor, your capacity to claim a tax deduction is limited to deriving assessable income such as your dividend payments. To satisfy this condition a share investor will need to check the company's dividend payment history to see whether there's a reasonable expectation the company will declare a dividend. Under the CGT provisions if your interest payments are not tax deductible, they can be included in the cost base of your shares, and can be taken into account when calculating a capital gain (see chapter 6). This will normally occur when you buy shares in companies that don't pay dividends.

 Tax tip

If the interest is prepaid and the prepaid period does not exceed 12 months, the interest is ordinarily tax deductible in the financial year you incur the expense. This is on the proviso that the purpose of the loan is to derive assessable income (for instance, dividends).

 Tax trap

If you borrow funds from a joint loan account (for instance, John and Betty's loan account) to buy shares in, say, John's name, or you borrow from an individual loan account (for instance, John's loan account) to buy shares in joint names (for instance, John and Betty), the interest payments you incur may not be fully tax deductible. If you intend to do this you should seek professional advice to ensure you claim the correct amount.

Borrowing costs

If you incur borrowing expenses to secure a loan (for instance, loan establishment fees, stamp duty and legal fees), you will need to spread the expenditure you incur over the period of the loan, or over five years (or more precisely 1826 days) if your loan exceeds the five-year limit. However, you can claim the amount outright if your borrowing costs do not exceed $100. The following formula is used to apportion your annual borrowing costs.

Borrowing costs × period in year ÷ total period of loan (maximum five years) = annual borrowing cost.

Case study: claiming a borrowing expense

On 1 October 2010 Charlie took out a loan over six years to fund the purchase of a share portfolio for the purpose of deriving dividends. The borrowing costs associated with setting up the loan amounted to $1200. As the purpose of the loan is to buy shares that generate dividends, the borrowing costs are tax deductible expenses. Because the amount exceeds $100, Charlie will need to spread the $1200 over the period of the loan or over five years (1826 days) if the loan exceeds five years. In this case, as the loan exceeds five years Charlie will need to apportion the $1200 borrowing expenses over five years as illustrated following:

Year	Annual borrowing cost
2011	$180 ($1200 × 273 days ÷ 1826 days)
2012	$240

2013	$240
2014	$240
2015	$240
2016	$60 (being the balance of tax deductible deduction)

If you take out a loan partway through the financial year (for instance, 1 October), you will have to pro-rate the amount you can claim in the first financial year you incur the expense (as illustrated in this case study).

Negative gearing

A term commonly associated with borrowing money to buy income-generating investments (such as a share portfolio) is negative gearing. When you negative gear you are effectively losing money (as your cash outflows will exceed your cash inflows). Under Australian tax law, if your tax deductible expenditure or cash outflows (primarily interest) exceed your dividend payments (cash inflows), you can deduct the net loss (net cash outflows) from other assessable income you derive (such as salary and wages, business profits and investment income). When this happens you'll reduce the tax payable on the other assessable income you derived, and at the same time reduce the loss by the amount of tax you saved. So it's important that you have another source of income to claim this loss, otherwise you could lose this tax benefit. This is especially the case if your taxable income is below $16 000 as no tax is payable (per 2010–11 tax rates).

Negative gearing can significantly benefit income earners who pay a high marginal rate of tax (for instance, 45 per cent). If you're contemplating negative gearing, keep in mind your shares must increase in value to cover the losses you incur while negative gearing. Otherwise, you could quickly find yourself paying off a loan to buy shares that are both decreasing in value and generating a negative cash flow. The following case study shows you how negative gearing works.

Case study: negative gearing a share portfolio

Brendan, a motor mechanic and share investor, borrowed $100 000 from the ANZ bank to buy a quality blue chip share portfolio. At the end of the financial year his accounting records showed he paid $7500 interest and received a $3000 fully franked dividend. The franking credit was $1286. He also incurred $300 expenditure in respect of deriving his dividends. Brendan also derived a $68 000 salary and his marginal rate of tax (plus Medicare levy) is 31.5 per cent. In chapter 5 it was pointed out when you receive a franked dividend you'll need to bring to account both the dividend and franking credit as part of your assessable income.

Negative gearing calculations

Dividends:

Franked amount	$3000	
Franking credit	$1286	$4286

Less:
Dividend and interest deductions:

Interest payments	$7500	
Dividend expenses	$300	$7800
Net loss (share portfolio)		$3514

Tax return for individuals

Salary or wages	$68000
Less:	
Net loss (share portfolio)	$3514
Taxable income	$64486

As Brendan had incurred a $3514 net loss from negative gearing his share portfolio, he can deduct this amount from the $68000 salary he derived. When he does this he will:

⇒ save paying tax on the salary he derived (as only $64486 is now taxable)

⇒ reduce the net loss by the amount of tax he saved.

Brendan's share portfolio will need to increase in value to cover the net loss from negative gearing his share portfolio. Otherwise, he will be paying off a loan to buy a share portfolio that is both decreasing in value and generating a negative cash flow.

Positive gearing

Positive gearing means your cash inflows (for instance, your dividend payments) are exceeding your cash outflows (for instance, your interest payments). In the meantime, if the shares you purchased increase in value you are indirectly getting paid for using someone else's money to make unrealised capital gains that won't be taxed until the shares are sold. So as long as your dividend payments exceed your interest payments and your shares are increasing in value, there would be no great urgency to sell your shares and/or terminate the loan agreement. Although you're liable to pay tax on your net dividend payments, you're not using any of your own funds while deriving an unrealised capital gain.

Case study: positive gearing a share portfolio

Tanya, a share investor, borrowed $50 000 to buy shares in ABC. The rate of interest is 7 per cent per annum, payable at the end of each month. Tanya's marginal rate of tax is 31.5 per cent. On 1 August she purchased 1000 ABC shares at $50 per share (total outlay $50 000).

On 15 August ABC declared a $1.30 interim dividend payable on 15 September (total payment $1300). Six months later ABC declared a $1.45 final dividend payable on 31 March (total payment $1450). On the cash outflow side of the equation, between 1 August and 31 March Tanya's interest payments amounted to $2333. When Tanya deducted her total interest payments ($2333) from her total dividend payments ($2750) she was $417 in front.

As Tanya's cash inflows (dividends) are exceeding her cash outflows (interest), she is positive gearing. When she found the market price of ABC on 31 March was $65.50 per share, she was $15 500 in front. So as long as Tanya's dividend payments exceed her interest payments and ABC continues to increase in value, there would be no urgency for her to sell the shares and/or terminate the loan agreement.

Although Tanya is liable to pay tax on the net dividend payment ($417), the $15 500 unrealised capital gain is not liable to tax until the shares are sold.

Personal loans

Personal loans are normally unsecured loans that you can take out to purchase a share portfolio. These loans can be structured as a fixed- or variable-rate loan. If the shares you purchase are likely to pay dividends your interest payments are a tax deductible expense. The dividends you receive can be used to help you service your loan repayments. If you take out an interest-only loan you will only be liable to pay back the interest during the term of the loan. If the interest is prepaid you can claim an upfront tax deduction (provided the prepaid period does not exceed 12 months), and you have the option to sell the shares when the loan matures. Taking out a personal loan is worth considering if you wish to participate in share purchase plans where you can purchase the shares at a discount. For this strategy to work to your advantage it's important that your shares appreciate in value. Otherwise you will be paying off a loan that's losing you money.

Case study: taking out a personal loan

Gino took out a 12-month personal loan to buy a share portfolio that's expected to pay a fully franked dividend. For this strategy to work, the shares he purchases will need to increase in value. If the interest is prepaid he can claim an upfront tax deduction in the financial year the expense is incurred. In the meantime Gino will derive a dividend and a franking credit, and when the loan matures he can sell the shares, repay the loan and pocket any capital gain on sale.

 Tax tip

The Australian Taxation Office has issued taxation ruling IT 2606: *Income tax: deduction for interest on borrowings to fund share acquisitions.* To obtain a copy of this ruling you can contact the ATO directly or you can visit its website <www.ato.gov.au>.

Margin lending

Margin lending is a borrowing facility where you'll use a mixture of your own capital and borrowings to purchase shares. Under this arrangement a margin lender will lend you funds up to a predetermined amount to buy approved Australian Securities Exchange (ASX) listed companies. In return you'll need to fund the balance by pledging some of your own capital (for instance, shares and/or cash). The maximum loan limit—called a loan-to-valuation ratio (LVR)—is normally set at around 70 per cent. For instance, if you buy a $100 000 share portfolio, the margin lender will provide 70 per cent of the funds (in this case $70 000), and you'll need to make up the balance ($30 000) in shares and/or cash. If you're carrying on a share trading business your interest payments are tax deductible (being a part of the cost of trading operations). If you're a share investor the interest is tax deductible only if the purpose of the loan is to derive assessable income such as dividends. If the interest is pre-paid 12 months in advance (for instance, in June) you can claim an upfront tax deduction at the end of the financial year. In the meantime, the tax you'll save from claiming a tax deduction and your dividend payments and franking credits will help you service your loan obligations.

If your shares increase in value you will be ahead, and no tax is payable on any unrealised capital gains until the shares are sold. But if your shares fall below a predetermined valuation you could be up for a margin call. If you get a margin call you'll need to inject additional shares and/or cash to cover the shortfall and restore the LVR. You'll normally need to do this within 24 hours. If you're unable to provide the necessary funds your shares will be sold, and if you are a share investor you'll incur a capital loss. Incidentally, margin lenders normally offer a buffer zone to allow for small daily fluctuations in the sharemarket. To reduce your exposure to a potential margin call you could consider borrowing less than the maximum permitted and invest in a diversified quality share portfolio.

Case study: margin loan

Vivian is a share investor who is keen to purchase a $100000 diversified blue chip share portfolio. To help finance the purchase she decides to take out a margin loan. Under this arrangement the margin lender will lend Vivian $70000 to buy listed shares the margin lender has agreed to finance. Vivian will need to use $30000 of her own capital to fund the balance. If the interest is prepaid she could qualify for an upfront tax deduction at the end of the financial year (provided the prepaid interest period does not exceed 12 months). The tax she'll save from claiming a tax deduction and the dividend payments and franking credits she's expected to receive will help her service the loan repayments.

If Vivian's shares increase in value she stands to make a capital gain if she sells them. But if her share portfolio decreases in value (for instance, from $100000 to $65000), she will get a margin call to cover the shortfall and restore the LVR. Incidentally, if Vivian incurs a margin call, the additional capital contribution is not a tax deductible expense. If Vivian can't come up with the necessary funds within 24 hours, her share portfolio will be sold and she will incur a capital loss.

Tax trap

In ATO interpretative decision ID 2007/58 the Tax Office ruled a trustee of a self managed superannuation fund (SMSF) that operated a margin account to purchase listed shares has contravened the *Superannuation Industry (Supervision) Act 1993*, as it has borrowed money and granted a charge over shares that are assets of the fund.

Line of credit

Under a line of credit facility a financial institution will agree to provide you with a predetermined credit limit to buy investments such as a share portfolio. It is similar in nature to an overdraft facility. If you use a line of credit to buy shares your interest payments are tax deductible to the extent it is incurred in gaining or producing assessable income or in carrying on a share trading business for that purpose.

A major benefit of this facility is you can quickly access funds up to your credit limit to take advantage of any good investment opportunities (for instance, a rights issue). Further, it's possible to take out an interest-only loan where your interest payment is the minimum amount you'll need to repay. Incidentally, interest is normally payable on a monthly basis. But you'll have the flexibility to make additional repayments. When you deduct your dividends from your interest payments you may find yourself positively gearing. This could happen when interest rates are low and you receive a dividend shortly after you buy your shares. If your shares fall in value there are no margin calls to restore the balance as is the case with a margin loan. On the other hand if your shares are increasing in value your unrealised capital gains are not liable to tax until they're sold.

Case study: line of credit

Angela, a share investor, has established a $40 000 line of credit to invest in the sharemarket. The facility was set up as a 7.5 per cent variable-rate interest-only loan, which means she is only required to repay the interest. But Angela has the flexibility to make additional repayments. She withdrew $30 000 to purchase 1000 PQR Ltd shares. Two months after she bought them the company paid her a $750 interim dividend fully franked and the market value of her shares had risen to $34.50. The amount of interest she paid amounted to $375, which is a tax deductible expense. If Angela were to sell the shares and repay the loan she will make a $4500 capital gain (less brokerage and GST). She will then be in the position to borrow up to $40 000 to buy more shares. In the meantime, if her shares were to fall below the purchase price she will not be up for a margin call.

Tax trap

If you have a split loan line of credit facility, where part of the loan is for private purposes (for instance, to repay your home mortgage) and part of the loan is to fund an investment portfolio (for instance, shares), you'll need to keep separate details of the arrangement. There are special rules relating to claiming a tax deduction in respect of your interest payments. The Tax Office has issued taxation ruling TR 2000/2: *Income tax: deductibility of interest on moneys drawn down under line of credit facilities and redraw facilities* to explain what you have to do. See also Tax Office publication *Split loan interest deductions*.

Capital protection loans

A capital protection loan is normally a limited non-recourse loan facility that you can use to finance the purchase of shares listed on the ASX. What makes this loan unique is you can protect yourself wholly or partly from incurring a potential loss if your shares fall below their purchase price. Under a non-recourse loan arrangement the lender rather than the investor suffers any potential loss on sale. As your shares are protected from a possible fall in value, the Tax Office treats the interest as if it were the payment of a put option. In chapter 8 I point out that a put option is similar to taking out insurance to protect yourself against a possible fall in the price of your shares.

As your interest payments will contain a capital protection component and a tax deductible interest component, your capacity to claim a tax deduction is limited to a benchmark interest rate (plus a further 1 per cent). The benchmark rate is the Reserve Bank of Australia's indicator rate for standard variable housing loans. Any payments that exceed this rate are treated as capital in nature and are not tax deductible. The good news here is under the CGT provisions the amount of interest that's disallowed (the cost of the capital protection component) can be included in the share's cost base. You can take this into account to calculate a capital gain on disposal of your shares (see chapter 6).

At a glance: capital protection loans

This is how a capital protection loan works:

- An investor can borrow funds to acquire shares listed on the ASX.

- The investor may be required to pledge some collateral (for instance, shares) to secure the loan.

- The investor will ordinarily be charged a high rate of interest plus capital protection fees. The interest can be prepaid to secure an upfront tax deduction (provided the prepaid interest period does not exceed 12 months).

- Put options are used to protect the lender if share prices fall (see chapter 8).

- The interest payments will contain a capital protection component and a tax deductible interest component.

- The investor's capacity to claim an interest deduction is limited to the Reserve Bank of Australia's indicator rate for standard variable housing loans (plus a further 1 per cent). Any non-deductible interest can be included in the share's cost base (see chapter 6).

- The investor will profit in a rising market while reducing their exposure to potential losses if share prices fall.

- If shares fall below their purchase price the investor can return them to the lender. The lender rather than the investor suffers any potential loss on sale. Because it is a non-recourse loan, the lender's capacity to recover any outstanding debts is limited to the value of the shares.

 Tax tip

If you want to know more about capital protection loans you can read Tax Office publication *How are capital protected products and borrowings treated?*

Instalment warrants

If you buy an instalment warrant you will have the right to buy shares in a company by making two instalment payments during the life of the warrant. Instalment warrants are normally issued by the major Australian banks. The first instalment payment (normally around 50 to 60 per cent of the cost of the shares) includes interest payable plus borrowing costs. The interest component is ordinarily a tax deductible expense (being incurred in the course of deriving your dividends), and your borrowing costs are tax deductible over the term of the loan. If the interest is prepaid and the prepaid period does not exceed 12 months, the interest is tax deductible in the financial year you incur the expense. The second instalment payment (balance payable) is normally due in 18 months' time. In the meantime the shares will be held in trust and ownership is transferred to you when you pay the second instalment.

Although you don't own the shares outright, under this arrangement you get to keep any dividends and franking credits the company declares, plus any capital growth if the shares appreciate in value. However, what makes this form of borrowing unique is you're not obligated to pay the second instalment. This could arise if the shares were to fall below the purchase price. If you do not pay the second instalment and you let the warrant lapse unexercised, you will forfeit the right to buy the shares. Ordinarily the shares will be sold and you may receive a portion of the net proceeds. Under the CGT provisions, as there is a disposal of a CGT asset you may derive a capital gain or incur a capital loss. In the meantime your instalment warrant can be traded on the ASX before the warrant's expiry date. For a comprehensive discussion on the taxation of warrants, visit the Australian Securities

Exchange website <www.asx.com.au>: go to 'Warrants' and read taxation article 'Taxation treatment of warrants'. Note also that specific taxation issues about a particular warrant may be provided by the issuer of the warrant.

Tax tip

A self managed superannuation fund (SMSF) is ordinarily prohibited from borrowing funds. Although instalment warrants is a form of borrowing, as from 24 September 2007 an SMSF can invest in instalment warrants provided it's in accordance with the fund's investment strategy. For more details read Tax Office publication *Instalment warrants and super funds—questions and answers* and Tax Office alert TA 2008/5: *Certain borrowings by self managed superannuation funds*.

Useful references

- Australian Securities & Investments Commission <www.fido.gov.au>; go to 'About financial products' and click on 'Loans & credit' and 'Margin loans'.

Australian Taxation Office publications

- *Deductions for prepaid expenses* (NAT 4170)

- *Instalment warrants*

- *What are capital protected products and borrowings?*

Australian Taxation Office interpretative decisions

- ID 2003/1119: *Income tax: timing of deductions for prepaid interest on money borrowed to acquire instalment warrants over stapled securities*

- ID 2007/58: *Superannuation: self managed superannuation fund: trustee using a margin account for fund investments in listed shares*

- ID 2009/71: *Income tax: deductions: interest expense on a loan to acquire options*

Other taxation rulings

- TR 2000/2: *Income tax: deductibility of interest on moneys drawn down under line of credit facilities and redraw facilities*

- TR 2004/4: *Income tax: deduction for interest incurred prior to the commencement of, or following the cessation of, relevant income earning activities*

- IT 2513: *Income tax: margin lending*

- IT 2606: *Income tax: deduction for interest on borrowings to fund share acquisitions*

Chapter 8

Taxation treatment of derivatives

A derivative is defined as a financial instrument that derives its value from the value of the underlying security (for instance, shares). The three most common ways of investing in derivatives are exchange traded options (ETOs), warrants and contracts for difference (CFDs). In this chapter I cover the general concepts and taxation issues associated with investing in these types of derivatives.

Exchange traded options

An exchange traded option gives you the right but not the obligation to buy or sell the underlying shares of a particular company at a predetermined price (exercise price) on or before the expiry date. Each contract size you will be dealing with is ordinarily 1000 shares. As you are only buying a 'right' you are not entitled to receive a dividend. There are over 70 companies that are linked with ETOs that you can trade on the Australian Securities Exchange (ASX). You can get a full list from the ASX website. An ETO is not created or issued by the individual companies. These options are created by an independent body and involve two parties referred to as the option taker and option writer.

If you want to trade in exchange traded options you will need to contact a stockbroker and complete a client agreement form. For more details you can read the Australian Securities Exchange publications *Understanding options trading* and *Margins*. You can get a copy of these publications from the ASX website <www.asx.com.au>.

Buying and selling a call and put option

There are two types of exchange traded options you can consider. They are a call option and put option. The price and expiry dates of the various exchange traded options you can buy or sell are published daily in the financial newspapers. You can also find them on the various online broker websites (see table 8.1).

The following sections explain how exchange traded options work.

Table 8.1: list of leading online brokers

Bell Direct	www.belldirect.com.au
CommSec	www.comsec.com.au
E*TRADE Australia	www.etrade.com.au
Macquarie Edge	www.macquarie.com.au/edge
OptionsXpress	www.optionsxpresss.com
Scottrade	www.scottrade.com
Share Builder	www.sharebuilder.com
TD Ameritrade	www.tdameritrade.com
Trade King	www.tradeking.com
Zecco Trading	www.zecco.com

Call option

Buying a call option gives the option taker the right (but not the obligation) to buy the underlying shares at a predetermined exercise price on or before the expiry date. When you buy a call option (referred to as 'opening a position') you will be anticipating that the price of the underlying shares will increase in value. So rather than buy the shares outright, for a small outlay (premium) you can buy a call option. The price of the premium will depend on the market price of the underlying shares you intend to buy and the period of time that's left (called time decay) before the call option expires. The size of each contract is ordinarily 1000 shares. You will find the price of your call option will rise and fall in line with the price movement of the underlying shares, and will become worthless on the expiry date.

There are three ways you can use a call option, namely:

- Exercise your right to buy the underlying shares at the exercise price on or before the expiry date.

- Sell the call option on the ASX before the expiry date by writing an identical option and derive a profit (or incur a loss) on the call option instead (referred to as 'closing out'). You will find this is normally the case as the majority of exchange traded options listed on the ASX are never exercised. The greater the shares increase in value the more profit you stand to make!

- Let the call option expire unexercised. If you don't exercise your right to buy the underlying shares by the expiry date the call option will expire worthless. The most you can lose is the premium you paid and you will incur a loss.

The person who receives the premium is the option writer. That person must sell the underlying shares to the option taker at the exercise price if the option taker exercises their right to buy on or before the expiry date. This will ordinarily occur if the underlying shares are trading above the exercise price. The option writer will be anticipating that the underlying shares will be trading below the exercise price on the expiry date. The writer of an option can close out their position prior to the expiry date by buying an identical option. The option writer will derive a profit if the call option expires unexercised.

Case study: call option

On 1 March Christine (option taker) is keen to buy 1000 BHP Billiton (BHP) shares, as there is a strong possibility they could increase in price within the next two months. BHP is currently trading at $37. Rather than buy the shares outright, she decides to pay a $1 premium (cost of call option) for the right, but not the obligation, to buy a BHP share for $40 on or before 30 April (date call option expires). As BHP is trading at $37 the call option is currently 'out of the money'. Christine is anticipating BHP will be trading above $41 ($40 exercise price plus the $1 premium) on or before 30 April.

If BHP increases to, say, $50, Christine is 'in the money' as she can exercise her right to buy 1000 BHP shares at $40. Alternatively, if the market value of her call option is trading at, say, $7, Christine can sell the option on the ASX and derive a $6 profit on sale ($7 sale price less $1 premium paid). On the other hand, if BHP were to fall to $29 Christine is out of the money. This is because it's unlikely she'll exercise her right to buy BHP at $40 when she can buy them on the open market for $29. Under these circumstances the most Christine will lose if the option expires unexercised is the $1 premium she paid and she will incur a loss.

If you're the option writer of a BHP call option you will receive the $1 premium from Christine (option taker). The risk here is you are now obligated to sell the specified number of BHP shares (in this case 1000) at the exercise price of $40 on or before

30 April if the option is exercised. This means if BHP increases to $50 and Christine exercises her right to buy BHP at $40, you as the option writer must sell the shares at $40 to Christine. Incidentally, if you do not own any BHP shares you will be said to be writing a 'naked' or 'uncovered' call option. If you do this and Christine exercises her call option, you must buy the required number of BHP shares on the open market (for instance, pay $50) and sell them to Christine at $40. But if BHP falls to $29 the option writer will derive a $1 profit. This is because it's unlikely Christine will pay $40 if the current market price is $29. In the meantime this call option can be sold on the ASX before the expiry date (close out).

Put option

If you own shares in a particular company and you consider they could fall in price, one way to protect your current position is to buy a put option. Buying a put option gives the option taker the right (but not the obligation) to sell their shares at the predetermined exercise price on or before the expiry date. This means if the market price of the underlying shares falls below the exercise price you can sell them at the exercise price. A put option is similar to taking out insurance to protect your position in a falling market. If you want to buy a put option you'll need to contact a stockbroker and pay a premium. Incidentally, as you are only buying a 'right to sell' you don't have to own the underlying shares. This means it's possible for you to profit merely from the price movement of the put option. So for this strategy to work to your advantage the price of the underlying shares must fall. You will find the price of your put option will rise and fall in line with the price movement of the underlying shares, and will become worthless on the expiry date.

There are three ways you can use a put option, namely:

- Exercise your right to sell the underlying shares to the option writer at the exercise price on or before the expiry date.

- Sell the put option on the ASX before the expiry date and derive a profit (or incur a loss) on the put option instead. The more the underlying shares decrease in value the more profit you stand to make!

- Let the put option expire unexercised. If you don't exercise your right to sell the underlying shares by the expiry date the put option will expire worthless. The most you can lose is the premium you paid and you will incur a loss.

The person who receives the premium (option writer) must buy the shares from the option taker at the exercise price. This will ordinarily occur if the underlying shares are trading below the exercise price. The option writer will be anticipating the underlying shares will either increase in value or stay relatively stable. As is the case with a call option, the price of the put option premium will depend on the current market price of the underlying shares, and the period of time that's left (time decay) before the put option expires. The writer of a put option can close out their position prior to the expiry date by buying an identical option. The option writer will derive a profit if the put option expires unexercised.

Tax tip

If you exercise your right to buy the shares (call option) the cost base will ordinarily include the exercise price plus the call option premium. According to Tax Office publication *What is the acquisition date of shares acquired by the exercise of an option? (Is it the date of the option being granted/ purchased or when the share is acquired?)*, the Tax Office has ruled the acquisition date is the date the share is acquired. This becomes an important issue for establishing the 12 months' ownership period for claiming the 50 per cent CGT discount. On the other hand, if you exercise your right to sell (put option), the option premium will ordinarily be deducted from the proceeds received on disposal of your shares.

Case study: put option

Mathew (option taker) owns 1000 Woolworths Ltd shares. The current market value on 1 September is $30. As there is a possibility they could fall in value within the next 30 days Mathew decides to buy a put option. The premium for the right but not the obligation to sell his Woolworths shares at $30 on or before 30 September is $1. If he finds two weeks later that Woolworths had fallen to $25, Mathew is 'in the money' as he can exercise his right to sell and will receive $30 (less the $1 premium he paid). On the other hand, if his Woolworths shares increase to $35 Mathew's put option is 'out of the money', as it's unlikely he will exercise his right to sell at $30, when he can sell them on the ASX for $35. Under these circumstances the most Mathew will lose if the option expires unexercised is the $1 premium he paid and he will incur a loss. But the good news here is he will benefit from a rising market. Mathew also has the option to sell the put option on the ASX before the put option expires (closes out).

If you're the option writer of a Woolworths put option you will receive the $1 premium from Mathew (option taker). The risk here is you are now obligated to buy the specified number of Woolworths Ltd shares (in this case 1000) at the exercise price of $30 on or before 30 September if the option is exercised. This means if Woolworths shares were to decrease to $25 and Mathew exercises his right to sell at $30, the option writer must buy the shares from Mathew at $30. Incidentally, as there are many option writers who received a premium for writing similar options, the Australian Clearing House will randomly select the option writer who must do this. On the other hand, if Woolworths shares increase to $35 the option writer will derive a $1 profit. This is because it's unlikely Mathew will exercise his right to sell at $30 when he can sell them on the ASX for $35. In the meantime this put option can be sold on the ASX before the put option expires (closes out).

At a glance: key elements of an exchange traded option

The following are terms/definitions that are commonly associated with exchange traded options:

- *Underlying shares:* restricted to the major Australian companies listed on the Australian Securities Exchange.

- *Exercise price:* the price you'll pay or receive for the underlying shares. Exchange traded options are normally American-style. This means you can exercise your right to buy or sell the underlying shares on or before the expiry date. If you can do this only on the expiry date the option is European-style.

- *Expiry date:* normally within 12 months of issue. On the expiry date the option will become worthless.

- *Contract size:* normally 1000 shares.

- *Premium:* the price you pay to participate or receive. It will rise or fall in line with the movement in the market price of the underlying shares.

- *Option taker:* the person who pays a premium for the right to buy or sell the underlying shares.

- *Option writer:* the person who receives the premium and must sell or buy the underlying shares if the option is exercised.

- *Australian Clearing House (ACH):* body responsible for registration and clearing of all exchange traded options.

Tax tip

The Australian Clearing House will calculate at the end of each trading day whether an option writer is liable to pay margin calls throughout the life of the option. This is to cover potential adverse price movements of the underlying shares, and to ensure the option writer will have sufficient cash to meet their legal obligations. This will arise if the option writer does not lodge the underling shares (or other acceptable securities) with their stockbroker as collateral to cover their commitments. These payments will be credited to the option writer's clearing house account. Under Australian tax law margin payments made in respect of exchange traded options are not tax deductible, as the payment is considered to be of a capital nature (for more details see tax determination TD 2006/25). Incidentally, if the writer of an option receives interest payments in respect of money held in their clearing house account, the interest payment will be treated as assessable income.

Taxation treatment of exchange traded options

The taxation treatment of exchange traded options will depend on whether you're carrying on a business trading in ETOs (commonly referred to as trading on revenue account) or you are a share investor (commonly referred to as trading on capital account); for more details see chapter 2.

If you carry on a business trading in exchange traded options you will be taxed as follows: the premiums receivable from that activity are ordinarily derived as assessable income at the time an ETO contract is registered with the ACH, whereas the premiums payable are ordinarily tax deductible expenses at the time an ETO contract is registered with the ACH.

On the other hand, if you are a share investor the premiums you receive or pay will fall for consideration under the CGT provisions. If the option expires worthless you may derive an assessable capital gain if you are the option writer or realise a capital loss if you are the option taker. For a comprehensive discussion on the taxation treatment of ETOs, visit the Australian Securities Exchange website <www.asx.com.au> and read 'Taxation treatment of exchange traded options'.

 Tax trap

The Tax Office has issued a ruling pointing out that exchange traded options do not fall within the definition of trading stock in accordance with the Income Tax Assessment Act. For more details see ATO interpretative decision ID 2004/526.

Checklist: key Australian Taxation Office rulings

The Tax Office has issued the following interpretative decisions and taxation determination in respect of specific issues relating to exchange traded options. As this area of the law can be complex you should seek professional advice if you're not sure what to do:

- ID 2004/526: *Income tax: options trading*

- ID 2005/164: *Capital gains tax: CGT event C2—close-out of an exchange traded option*

- ID 2006/313: *Income tax: share option trading*

- ID 2009/53: *Income tax: derivation of an amount received on the cash settlement of an exercised option*

- ID 2009/54: *Income tax: deductibility of an amount paid on the cash settlement of an exercised option*

- ID 2009/55: *Income tax: deductibility of premiums payable on the acquisition of options*

- ID 2009/56: *Income tax: assessability of premiums receivable on the sale of options*

- ID 2009/57: *Income tax: exchange traded options: derivation of premiums receivable*

- ID 2009/58: *Income tax: exchange traded options: deductibility of premiums payable*

- ID 2009/59: *Income tax: shares acquired and disposed of in an options trading business: trading stock*

- ID 2009/71: *Income tax: deductions: interest expense on a loan to acquire options*

- ID 2009/110 *Income tax: self managed superannuation funds: exchange traded options—tax treatment of premiums receivable*

- ID 2009/111 *Income tax: self managed superannuation funds: exchange traded options — tax treatment of premiums payable*

- TD 2006/25: *Income tax: are margin payments made in respect of exchange traded option and futures contracts deductible under section 8-1 of the* Income Tax Assessment Act 1997?

 Tax tip

The Tax Office has issued a ruling pointing out that where a self managed superannuation fund writes an ETO as part of a hedging strategy, the premiums receivable from that activity are assessable under the capital gains tax provisions. For more details see ATO interpretative decision ID 2009/110.

Warrants

Buying and selling a warrant is similar in nature to trading in exchange traded options. The only difference here is that the transaction is between the purchaser and issuer of the warrant (rather than between an option taker and option writer). Warrants are normally issued by Australia's major banks and financial institutions, including:

- Credit Suisse
- Challenger Equities Ltd

- Commonwealth Bank of Australia Ltd
- Macquarie Bank Ltd
- Merrill Lynch International and Co
- SG Australia Ltd
- Westpac Banking Corporation Ltd.

For a comprehensive list of warrant issuers you can visit the ASX website <www.asx.au> and read fact sheet 'Warrant issuer contact sheet'.

A warrant gives you the right but not the obligation to buy from the warrant issuer or sell to the warrant issuer the underlying shares (for instance, BHP Billiton) at a predetermined exercise price, on or before the date the warrant expires. The life of a warrant normally does not exceed 12 months. The amount of shares you can buy (or sell) depends on a conversion ratio. For instance, if the conversation ratio is 2:1 it means you'll need to buy two warrants for the right to buy one share. Alternatively, you can sell the warrant on the ASX before it expires. Settlement can be either a cash payment or the physical delivery of the underlying shares.

Warrants can be either American-style warrants or European-style warrants. If you can exercise your right to buy (or sell) the warrant at any time prior to the expiry date, the warrant is an American-style warrant. If you can exercise your right to buy (or sell) the warrant only on the expiry date, the warrant is a European-style warrant.

Tax tip

It's possible for you to speculate in the price movements of foreign currencies (commonly known as forex). If you plan to do this (or you intend to buy and sell shares in foreign countries) the Tax Office has issued a number of publications in respect of the tax issues you'll need to take into account. The main ones are listed here:

⇒ *Foreign exchange*

⇒ *Foreign exchange (forex): overview*

⇒ *Foreign exchange (forex): questions and answers*

⇒ *Foreign exchange (forex): foreign currency denominated bank accounts*

⇒ *Foreign exchange (forex): foreign currency denominated shares*

⇒ *Foreign exchange (forex): hedging transactions*

⇒ *Foreign exchange (forex): acquisition of a CGT asset*

⇒ *Foreign exchange (forex): realisation event ordering rules*

You can get these publications from the Tax Office website <www.ato.gov.au>. As these issues can be complicated it is recommended that you seek professional advice.

Before you invest in a warrant, you should read the terms and risks associated with the particular warrant series you intend to purchase. The necessary details are set out in a document called an 'Offering Circular'. Alternatively, you can contact the warrant issuer directly or a stockbroker for specific details.

There are many different types of warrants you can buy (for instance, equity warrants, instalment warrants, endowment warrants, capital plus warrants, low exercise price warrants and capped warrants). Details of the various warrants currently on the market are published in financial newspapers and on the ASX website. The two most popular warrants you can buy are equity warrants (discussed following) and instalment warrants (discussed in chapter 7).

Equity warrants

There are two types of equity warrants that you can buy and sell. They are call warrants and put warrants, and are similar in nature to exchange traded call and put options. The one you'll select depends on whether you consider the share price of a particular company is likely to rise or fall within a given period of time. For instance, if you buy a call warrant you will be anticipating the share price will rise, and if you buy a put warrant you will be anticipating the share price will fall.

Call warrant

A call warrant gives the buyer the right but not the obligation to buy the underlying shares from the warrant issuer at a predetermined price on or before the expiry date. As mentioned previously, when you buy a call warrant you will be anticipating that the market price of the underlying shares will be trading above the exercise price. For instance, if the exercise price is $12 and you find before the warrant expires that the market price of the underlying shares is $15, you can exercise your right to buy them at $12. Alternatively, rather than exercise your right to buy the underlying shares, you can sell the call warrant on the ASX before it expires and derive a profit on the warrant.

Tax tip

If you exercise your right to buy the underlying shares, the cost base of the shares you acquire will include your acquisition costs (for instance, brokerage fees and the premium you paid for the warrant) plus the price you paid for the shares. Incidentally, there are no CGT issues to worry about at the time you exercise your right to buy the underlying shares. You will be considered to have acquired the underlying shares at the time you exercise your right to buy them.

If the market price of the underlying shares falls below the exercise price, the call warrant will fall in value and will become worthless on the expiry date. For instance, if the exercise price of the underlying shares is $10 and the market price falls to $6, it's unlikely you will exercise your right to buy the shares from the warrant issuer for

$10 when you can buy them for $6 on the ASX. The most you'll lose is the premium you paid to purchase the call warrant and you will incur a loss.

Case study: buying a call warrant

On 15 March Julia is of the opinion that Westpac Banking Corporation (WBC) shares will increase in price within the next six months. The shares are currently trading at $28.70. Rather than buy the shares outright Julia decides to buy a call warrant. She examines the daily newspapers and decides to buy the following call warrant issued by Macquarie Bank Ltd.

Issuer: Macquarie Bank Ltd

European-style warrant

Exercise price	$30
Expiry date	24 September
Conversion ratio	1:1
Bid price	$0.14
Offer price	$0.15

European-style means you can exercise your right to buy the underlying shares from Macquarie Bank Ltd at the exercise price of $30 on the expiry date (24 September) only. The conversion ratio 1:1 means you'll need to buy one warrant for the right to buy one WBC share at the exercise price of $30 on 24 September. The bid price ($0.14) is the price a buyer is willing to pay for a warrant, and the offer price ($0.15) is the price a seller is prepared to sell the warrant to you.

On 15 March Julia purchases 10000 WBC call warrants at $0.15 per warrant (total outlay $1500). As the warrant is a European-style warrant Julia can exercise her right to buy 10000 WBC shares from Macquarie Bank Ltd on the expiry date (24 September) only. At this point in time Julia's call warrants are 'out of the money', as the market price of a WBC share ($28.70) is below the exercise price ($30). Before Julia will be ahead, WBC will need to be trading above $30.15 (exercise price $30 plus the $0.15 premium Julia paid for the warrant) on the expiry date.

On 12 September WBC is trading at $32.10 and the bid price of the call warrant has risen to $2.12 (the difference between the current market price ($32.10) and exercise price ($30) plus a further $0.02 cents because the warrant has not yet expired—referred to as time decay). As Julia is 'in the money' and there's a risk the shares could fall between 12 September and 24 September, she decides to sell the call warrants on the ASX for $2.12 and receives $21200 for them. She derived a $19700 profit during the time she owned the call warrants [($2.12 – $0.15) × 10000].

If the market price of WBC were to fall to $20 on the expiry date Julia's call warrant will expire worthless. This is because it's unlikely Julia will exercise her right to buy the shares from the warrant issuer for $30 when she can buy them on the ASX for $20. The most Julia will lose is the $1500 premium and she will incur a loss.

Put warrant

When you buy a put warrant you will have the right, but not the obligation, to sell the underlying shares at the exercise price to the warrant issuer, on or before the expiry date. A put warrant will allow you to protect your current position if your shares were to fall in value before the put warrant expires. For instance, if the exercise price of the underlying shares is $17 and their current market price is $14 you will be 'in the money', as you can exercise your right to sell the shares at $17 to the issuer of the put warrant. Alternatively, you can sell your put warrant on the ASX before it expires and derive a profit on the put warrant. Incidentally, as you are only buying a 'right to sell' you don't have to own the underlying shares. This means it's possible for you to merely profit from the price movement of the put warrant between the dates you buy the warrant and the expiry date. Remember, for this strategy to work to your advantage the price of the underlying shares must fall below the exercise price.

If the market price of the underlying shares were to rise above the exercise price, your put warrant will fall in price (as you will be 'out of the money') and will become worthless on the expiry date. For instance, if the exercise price is $17 and the market price increases to $20, it's unlikely you'll sell your shares to the issuer for $17, when you can sell them for $20 on the ASX. The most you'll lose is the premium you paid to purchase your put warrant and you will incur a loss.

Case study: buying a put warrant

Setanta is of the opinion that BHP Billiton (BHP) shares could fall in value over the next six weeks. On 3 February the market price of BHP shares is $40.54. To take advantage of a possible fall in price Setanta decides to buy a put warrant. He examines the various put warrants currently on the market and decides to buy the following:

Issuer: CBA Ltd
American-style warrant

Exercise price	$38.40
Expiry date	15 March
Conversion ratio	1:1
Bid price	$0.14
Offer price	$0.15

As this put warrant is an American-style warrant, for an outlay of $0.15 Setanta will have the right but not the obligation to sell one BHP share to CBA Ltd and receive $38.40 on or before 15 March. The conversion ratio 1:1 means he'll need to buy one put warrant in order to sell one BHP share. As BHP is currently trading above the exercise price ($38.40) the put warrant is currently 'out of the money'. Setanta decides to buy 10000 put warrants (total outlay $1500). On 6 March BHP has fallen to $34.56, and the value of his put warrant has subsequently risen to $3.86 (the difference between the exercise price ($38.40) and market price ($34.56) plus a further $0.02 cents 'time decay' because the warrant has not yet expired). As his put warrant is now 'in the money', Setanta can do one of two things.

⇛ He can sell his BHP shares to the issuer (CBA) and receive $38.40 per share (he could then buy the shares back on the ASX at $34.56); or

⇛ He can sell the put warrant on the ASX. If he does this he will derive a $37 100 profit on sale [($3.86 – $0.15) × 10 000].

On the other hand, if BHP is trading above the exercise price (for instance, $41.00) the most Setanta will lose is the premium he paid (namely $1500) and he will incur a loss.

Taxation treatment of warrants

The taxation treatment of warrants is similar to that of exchange traded options, discussed in the previous section. The way you'll be taxed will depend on whether you're carrying on a business trading in warrants or you are a share investor (see chapter 2). If you are carrying on a business trading in warrants any profits you derive will ordinarily be included as part of your assessable income and any losses you incur would ordinarily be an allowable deduction. On the other hand, if you're a share investor a capital gain or capital loss from a warrant transaction would fall for consideration under the CGT provisions. For further information you can visit the Australian Securities Exchange website and read 'Income tax treatment of warrants'. Also, specific taxation issues about a particular warrant may be provided by the issuer of the warrant.

Contracts for difference

A contract for difference (CFD) is a derivative that allows you to speculate in the price movement of underlying securities (for instance, shares) without owning the security. Contracts for difference were introduced in Australia in 2002 and are ordinarily short-term contracts (for instance, one week) between a buyer and CFD provider. The major CFD providers that deal with these financial instruments are:

- CMC Markets

- CommSec

- E*TRADE Australia

- IG Markets

- MQ Prime.

Under a contract for difference agreement, both parties to the contract will take an opposite view: you will be effectively betting (speculating) whether the value of the underlying security (shares) is likely to increase or decrease in value. If you want to participate you'll need to pay a deposit (normally 10 per cent) into the CFD provider's account and borrow the balance from the CFD provider. So for a small outlay it's possible for you to make a substantial profit if you get a favourable outcome. But you can also lose a substantial amount as well. The interest payments are calculated daily and you will incur brokerage fees. You could also be liable to margin calls to cover any potential losses on open positions. Settlement is a cash payment which is the difference between the opening and closing price of the shares. The buyer has no right to the delivery of the shares. On the settlement date the buyer will repay the amount borrowed. If the outcome for the buyer is positive (the buyer had correctly anticipated the shares would either rise or fall), the CFD provider will pay the difference. Under these circumstances the buyer will derive a profit. Conversely, if the outcome on the settlement date is negative, the buyer will pay the difference to the CFD provider and will incur a loss. To reduce the risk of incurring substantial losses the buyer can enter into a guaranteed stop-loss arrangement that will limit any potential loss to a predetermined amount.

Case study: buying a contract for difference

The current market price of ABC Ltd is $10.50. Kristen is of the view that the company is likely to increase in value within the next week. She contacts a CFD provider and purchases 10000 CFDs (total value $105000). She pays a 10 per cent deposit into the CFD provider's account and borrows the balance from the CFD provider. The interest payable is 8 per cent calculated daily. She also incurs buy and sell brokerage fees and GST. Kristen closes the contract three days later when the shares have increased 50 cents in value and makes a $4400 profit after payment of transaction costs and interest charges (see calculations overleaf). The return on her investment is 41.9 per cent ($4400 ÷ $10500 × 100).

Calculations

Opening value	$105 000
Less:	
Closing value	$110 000
Difference	$5 000
Less:	
Brokerage fees, GST and interest charges	$600
Net profit on trade	$4 400

On the other hand, if ABC Ltd had fallen 50 cents in value Kristen would have incurred a $5000 loss plus brokerage fees, GST and interest charges.

Taxation treatment of contracts for difference

Under Australian tax law, if you carry on a business trading in contracts for difference or you enter into the transaction for the purpose of profit-making (which is usually the case), any gain you derive or loss you incur will be treated as assessable income or an allowable deduction. All of this of course is a question of fact.

In the unlikely event the facts suggest this is not the case, you could be liable to pay tax under the CGT provisions. This is because financial contracts for difference come within the definition of a CGT asset, and a CGT event will arise when the contract is closed out. As a consequence any gain or loss would be assessable or deductible under the CGT provisions. However, the

Tax Office has stated in a tax ruling that if you enter into a financial contract for difference *for the purpose of recreation by gambling,* any capital gain or capital loss will be disregarded under the CGT-exempt gambling provisions. This could turn out to be a great decision if you make a capital gain, as no tax is payable. But trying to prove to the ATO that it's on capital account is another story! The bad news here is if you make a capital loss you will not be able to offset the capital loss against a capital gain.

 Tax tip

The Tax Office's views on the taxation treatment of financial contracts for difference are set out in tax ruling TR 2005/15: *Income tax—tax consequences of financial contracts for differences.* You can download a copy from the ATO website <www.ato.gov.au>.

 Tax trap

The Tax Office points out in tax ruling TR 2005/15, 'Although it is not possible to exclude (as a matter of law) the possibility that a financial contract for differences will be entered into for some purpose that is neither profit-making nor recreational, it is (as a matter of fact) considered to be "exceedingly unlikely"'. So if you incur a capital loss it is 'exceedingly unlikely' you can claim it!

Useful references

- Australian Securities Exchange (www.asx.com.au) —go to 'ASX listed CFDs'.

- Australian Securities Exchange derivatives division publications:

  □ *Understanding options trading*

  □ *Understanding options strategies*

  □ *Warrants—understanding trading and investment warrants*

Australian Taxation Office publications

- *Rights or options to acquire shares or units*

- *What is the acquisition date of shares acquired by the exercise of an option?*

Australian Taxation Office interpretative decisions

- ID 2007/56: *Superannuation: self managed superannuation funds: contracts for differences (CFDs)—no fund assets deposited with CFD provider*

- ID 2007/57: *Superannuation: self managed superannuation funds: contracts for differences (CFDs)—fund assets deposited with CFD provider—charge over fund assets*

- ID 2010/7: *Income tax: self managed superannuation funds: tax treatment of futures contracts*

Other taxation rulings

- TD 2006/25: *Income tax: are margin payments made in respect of exchange-traded option and futures contracts deductible under section 8-1 of the* Income Tax Assessment Act 1997?

- TR 2004/D17: *Income tax and capital gains tax: tax consequences of financial contracts for differences*

- TR 2005/15: *Income tax: tax consequences of financial contracts for differences*

- GSTD 2005/3: *Goods and services tax: are contracts for difference and financial spread betting contracts financial supplies?*

Chapter 9

Keeping proper records and tax audits

Investors who own shares and share traders who carry on a share trading business are required to maintain proper records of all their share trading activities. Penalties will apply if you fail to comply with this legal obligation. In this chapter I emphasise the need to keep proper records and explain what happens if the Australian Taxation Office were to audit your tax return.

Record-keeping

Under Australian tax law you must keep your records for five years after you lodge your annual tax return for individuals. According to the Tax Act your records must be kept in the English language and must be readily available for inspection in the event of a tax audit.

Tax tip

Under Australian tax law the Tax Office has full and free access to all buildings, places, books and documents and other papers for the purposes of the Tax Act, and can make extracts from or copies of any such books, documents or papers. The Tax Office also has the power to compel you to supply any relevant information for the purposes of the Tax Act.

What you'll need to keep

You will need to retain the following records relating to your share trading activities, and will need to produce these records if you're audited by the Australian Taxation Office.

Shareholder dividend statements

These documents will set out all the unfranked dividends, franked dividends and franking credits you derive each financial year (see chapter 5, figure 5.1, p. 71). You should record the relevant details on a spreadsheet in strict date order as set out in figure 9.1.

Figure 9.1: summary of dividends received

SUMMARY OF DIVIDENDS RECEIVED

Year Ended 30 June 20XX

Account Name: Eddy Simpson

Company name	Date paid	Unfranked	Franked	Franking credit	Grossed-up amount
BAN Ltd	10-Jul-00	$147.90	$1 331.10	$570.47	$2 049.47
XYZ Ltd	19-Sep-00		$817.60	$350.40	$1 168.00
GFD Ltd	28-Sep-00		$200.00	$85.71	$285.71
ABC Ltd	10-Oct-00		$13 410.00	$5 747.14	$19 157.14
BAN Ltd	2-Feb-XX		$1 805.00	$773.57	$2 578.57
XYZ Ltd	4-Apr-XX		$10 735.00	$4 600.71	$15 335.71
ABC Ltd	19-May-XX		$10 000.00	$4 285.00	$14 285.00
		$147.90	$38 298.70	$16 413.00	$54 859.60

At the end of the financial year you can transfer the total amounts to your tax return for individuals at Item 12: Dividends. Further, you can quickly transfer the relevant details to your business activity statement or instalment activity statement if you are required to submit one to the Tax Office.

Tax tip

Under the pay-as-you-go system you may be required to prepare a business activity statement or instalment activity statement setting out the amount of dividends you derive and/or share sales you do and pay tax on an ongoing basis. You'll need to keep accurate records of your dividends and share sales to comply with this legal requirement. The Tax Office will notify you whether you'll need to do this.

Buy contract notes

You must retain all the buy contract notes you receive from your stockbroker at the time you buy your shares. These documents will summarise all the relevant details of your share purchases (see chapter 3). You will need to retain these documents for the purposes of calculating whether you had made a capital gain or capital loss at the time you sell your shares. If you misplace or accidentally destroy your buy contact notes (and/or sell contract notes) you can contact your stockbroker for a duplicate copy. With respect to your buy contract notes, keep in mind the following key points:

- You are considered to have purchased your shares at the time of the making of the contract (purchase date) rather than on the settlement date.

- Each time you purchase identical shares in the same company on different occasions, they are treated as separate CGT assets with different cost bases and purchase dates. So it's important that you're able to distinguish the different parcels of shares you buy or sell. You'll need to know this for the purposes of working out whether you had made a capital gain or capital loss. Your buy contract notes will help you to make this distinction (see chapter 6).

- If you are a share investor it's recommended that you record all your share transactions on a spreadsheet in strict date order as set out in figure 9.2 (overleaf). This will conveniently summarise all your purchases and sales and the profit or loss you made on disposal. These details can be taken directly from your buy and sell contract notes. This will help you to see at a glance all the share trades you had conducted over the years and whether you had made a profit or loss. You should also keep a separate record of each company you currently hold as set out in figure 9.3 (on p.184). The relevant details were taken from the buy and sell contract notes in chapter 3 and more particularly figure 3.1 and figure 3.3.

Figure 9.2: summary of share transactions

Account name: Eddy Simpson

Purchase date	Sale date	Quantity	Company	Purchase price	Sale price	Profit/loss	Comments
Year ended 30 June 20PP							
12-Jul-OO		5000	ABC Ltd	$8941.58			
13-Jul-OO		24	BAN Ltd				Dividend reinvestment plan
16-Aug-OO		4000	XYZ Ltd	$14916.92			
	20-Sep-OO	550	DEC Ltd		$1666.90	$71.90	Non-discount capital gain
	01-Oct-OO	200	EFG Ltd		$6189.40	$4329.21	Non-discount capital gain
	05-Dec-OO	4000	HIJ Ltd		$16764.23	−$2723.06	Capital loss
15-Feb-PP		500	ABC Ltd	$11915.82			
26-Jun-PP		3000	XYZ Ltd	$9242.56			
End of financial year summary						$1678.05	

Year ended 30 June 20QQ						
13-Jul-PP	20	BAN Ltd				Dividend reinvestment plan
10-Sep-PP	4000	XYZ Ltd		$19 682.92	$4 766.00	Discount capital gain
7-Oct-PP	3000	ABM Ltd		$15 724.72	$4 157.48	Non-discount capital gain
24-Nov-PP	4000	ABC Ltd	$13 647.07			
20-Feb-PP	1000	PQR Ltd				
18-Apr-QQ	5000	ABC Ltd		$6 295.40	-$2 646.18	Capital loss
17-May-QQ	1000	BBH Ltd				
13-Jun-QQ	840	XPP Ltd				
End of financial year summary					$6 277.30	
Year ended 30 June 20RR						
21-Jul-XX	1000	Apex Ltd	$15 550.00			
18-Oct-XX	1000	Apex Ltd		$21 400.00	$5 850.00	Non-discount capital gain

Figure 9.3: record of share holdings

Apex Ltd

Account Name: Eddy Simpson

	Buy contract note					Sell contract note						
Date	Units purchased	Purchase details	Total cost	Contract number	Date	Units sold	Sale details	Net proceeds	Contract number	Net gain/ net loss	Comments
21-July-20XX	1000	1000 @ $15.45	$15450.00	42697401	18-Oct-20XX	1000	1000 @ $21.50	$21500.00	84192367		Non-discount capital gain
		Brokerage & GST	$100.00				Brokerage & GST	-$100.00			
			$15550.00					$21400.00		$5850.00	

If you are a share trader you should record the details of your purchases and sales in two separate spreadsheets as illustrated in chapter 3.

Holding statements

Keep all the holding statements you receive from the company. This document will set out the number of shares you own and is prima facie proof of ownership (see chapter 3, figure 3.2). If you contact the company's share registry you will need to quote your holder identification number or security reference number (see chapter 3). As this document does not provide any specific details of the shares you purchase, you should keep your holding statements with the corresponding buy contract notes you receive from your stockbroker.

 Tax tip

To help you maintain proper records you can set up a CGT asset register to help you keep track of all the shares you intend to keep for a long period of time. If you want to do this, the information will need to be certified by a registered tax agent or a person approved by the Tax Office. For more details you can read Tax Office publication *Guide to capital gains tax* (NAT 4151) and more particularly go to the section 'Keeping records—asset registers'. You can download a copy from the Tax Office website <www.ato.gov.au>.

Deductible expenses

You will need to keep relevant receipts and documents to verify and substantiate any expenses you incur in deriving your dividends (for instance, interest on borrowings). If you carry on a business as a share trader you can claim expenses that are necessarily incurred in respect of deriving assessable income (trading profits) that are not normally available to share investors (see chapter 5).

Calculations

You must keep a record of how you calculated any capital gains or capital losses you made on disposal of your shares. I discuss how you calculate a capital gain or capital loss in detail in chapter 6. Incidentally, you will find in Tax Office publication *Guide to capital gains tax* a capital gain or capital loss worksheet that you can use to help you to correctly calculate a capital gain or capital loss.

In chapter 6 it was pointed out if you incur a capital loss, you can only deduct it from a capital gain. If you make no capital gains your capital losses can be offset against future capital gains. You will need to keep an accurate record of all the capital losses not yet recouped. If you have unapplied capital losses from earlier years, you must offset any capital gain you make against the earlier years in the order you incur your capital losses. For instance, if you incurred a capital loss two years ago and a further capital loss one year ago, any capital gain you derive must first be applied against the capital loss you incurred two years ago and then against the capital loss you incurred one year ago.

Sell contract notes

When you sell your shares your stockbroker will issue a sell contract note setting out the amount of shares you sold, the date you sold them and the net proceeds on sale (see chapter 3, figure 3.3). Keep in mind that under the CGT provisions you will be considered to have sold your shares at the time of the making of the contract (sale date) rather than on the settlement date when you receive the net proceeds. As mentioned previously, it's recommended that you record the details of sale in the 'summary of share transactions' as set out in figure 9.2, and keep a separate record of each company you currently hold as set out in figure 9.3. You'll need to keep your sell contract notes to verify your capital gains or capital losses on sale, and all your assessable sales if you're carrying on a business as a share trader.

Tax tip

If you need specific details about your share transactions (or you inherit shares from a deceased estate), you can visit your company's share registry website. Two major share registry services that deal with the registration of shares are Link Market

Tax tip (cont'd)

Services Limited <www.linkmarketservices.com.au> and Computershare Investor Services Pty Limited <www-au.computershare.com/investor>. You can contact the company if you're not sure which service your company belongs to. To do this you'll need to quote your holder identification number (HIN) or security reference number (SRN).

Tax audits

In chapter 1 it was pointed out Australia operates under a self-assessment basis. Under this system, when you lodge your tax return the Tax Office will ordinarily accept its contents as being true and correct. Nevertheless, the Tax Office reserves the right to audit your tax affairs. When a tax audit takes place the Tax Office will examine all your records to check whether the information you had disclosed in your tax return is in accordance with your personal records. With respect to your share transactions they will normally check the following:

- whether all your dividends have been disclosed

- whether you have claimed the correct amount of franking credits

- whether you have kept proper receipts to verify and substantiate all your expenses

- whether you have correctly calculated your capital gains or capital losses

- if you are a share trader, whether you have correctly accounted for all your trading sales and purchases (as per your buy and sell contract notes).

If any errors are detected (for instance, you understated your income and/or overstated your expenses), your tax return will be amended and penalties may apply.

 Tax trap

Keep in mind the Tax Office performs ongoing dividend checks by comparing the information you had or had not disclosed in your tax return with all the companies' dividend payment records. Chances are the system will eventually find you out if you fail to disclose the correct amount of dividends and franking credits in your tax return. For more details see Tax Office publication *Share market transactions data matching*.

Under Australian tax law the Tax Office has the power to amend an assessment. Generally, there is a time limit of between two and four years from the date the tax became due and payable. Conversely, you also have the right to seek an amendment (for instance, you forgot to claim some expenses). You can also lodge an objection if you are dissatisfied with a Tax Office's decision or your notice of assessment. You also have the right to appeal to the Administrative Appeals Tribunal — Small Taxation Claims Tribunal or Tax Appeals Division.

Useful references

Australian Taxation Office publications

- *Keeping your tax records*
- *Record keeping for CGT*
- *Records relating to shares and units*
- *Sale of shares (supporting document requirements for objections)*
- *Tax audits — what are they?*

Other taxation rulings

- TR 2002/10: *Income tax: capital gains tax: asset register*
- TR 96/7: *Income tax record keeping — section 262A — general principles*

Glossary

All Ordinaries index An index used to measure the movements in Australian share prices. It comprises the top 500 companies listed on the Australian Securities Exchange and represents 99 per cent of total market capitalisation.

allowable deductible An expense you can deduct from your assessable income.

American-style This means the holder of an equity option or equity warrant has the right to buy or sell the underlying shares at any time up to the expiry date.

annual general meeting Yearly meeting of shareholders to discuss the performance of the company as set out in the annual report, to vote on certain issues and to elect company directors.

annual report   A report prepared by the directors of a company setting out the company's financial accounts and a summary of its performance.

application form   A form attached to a prospectus, which you will need to complete if you want to invest money in a particular company or managed fund.

assessable income   This is income you derive that is liable to tax. Assessable income consists of ordinary income and statutory income (per Australian taxation legislation).

Australian Clearing House (ACH)   Body responsible for registration and clearing of all exchange traded options.

Australian Securities Exchange (ASX) This is Australia's major market securities exchange responsible for regulating and controlling the buying and selling of Australian listed securities such as shares.

Australian Taxation Office (ATO)   Federal government authority responsible for administering the Income Tax Assessment Act.

beneficiary   A person entitled to receive a distribution from a trust.

bid   The price you are prepared to pay for shares in a company.

blue chip   An established company that is trading profitably.

bonus shares   Free shares issued by a company. The amount you'll receive is normally in proportion to your current share holdings; for instance, if a company declares a one-for-five bonus issue you will receive one free share for every five you own.

brokerage fee   The charge you incur from a stockbroker when you buy or sell shares. It's calculated on a percentage of the market price of the shares at the time you buy or sell.

business activity statement   A statement under the pay-as-you-go system that you prepare at the end of each reporting period (usually quarterly) disclosing certain income that is liable to tax.

buy contract note   An invoice you receive from a stockbroker at the time you buy shares. It will summarise the details of the transaction and can be used to calculate a capital gain or capital loss for taxation purposes.

call option   This gives the holder the right, but not the obligation, to buy the underlying shares at an agreed price on or before the expiry date. A call option is worth buying in a rising market.

call warrant   This gives the holder the right, but not the obligation, to buy the underlying shares from the issuer (usually a bank) at an agreed price on or before the expiry date. A call warrant is worth buying in a rising market.

capital   Funds used to conduct business operations. Also money invested in assets such as shares.

capital gain   A gain you make when you sell CGT assets such as shares for a price that's greater than their cost base. Under Australian tax law a capital gain is liable to capital gains tax. The way you calculate a capital gain changed on 21 September 1999.

capital gains tax (CGT)   A tax on capital gains you make on disposal of CGT assets such as shares that you acquire on or after 20 September 1985.

capital growth   An increase in the value of your investment.

capital loss   The loss you incur when you sell CGT assets such as shares for a price that's below their reduced cost base. Under Australian tax law a capital loss can only be offset against a capital gain.

capital proceeds   The sale price of a CGT asset such as shares.

capital protection loan   A loan to buy shares where you can protect yourself from incurring a loss if your share portfolio falls in value. These are normally non-recourse loans where the lender rather than the investor suffers any potential loss. You will be charged a high rate of interest.

CGT asset   An asset such as shares that's liable to tax under the capital gains tax provisions.

CGT asset register   A register you keep to record all CGT assets you own such as your share portfolio.

CGT event   Normally arises when there's a change in ownership of a CGT asset such as shares (for instance, when you sell them or gift them to someone).

CHESS   Short for Clearing House Electronic Sub-register System. This is a system to keep track of share transactions. You will be issued with a holder identification number (HIN) and your stockbroker will use this number whenever shares are bought and sold on your behalf.

company   A separate legal entity that can carry on a business in its own name. A company raises capital to fund its business operations through the issue of shares. A company pays a 30 per cent rate of tax. (At the time of writing, the Federal Labor Government has proposed to reduce the rate to 29 per cent in the 2013–14 financial year and to 28 per cent in the 2014–15 financial year.)

complying superannuation fund   A fund that has elected to be regulated under the Superannuation Industry (Supervision) Act. Complying super funds are taxed at the rate of 15 per cent and can pay pensions to their members.

condition of release   A condition you must satisfy before you can access your benefits in a superannuation fund. The most common condition is when you retire.

consumer price index (CPI)   An index that Australia uses to calculate its rate of inflation.

contract for difference (CFD)   A derivative that allows you to speculate in the price movement of underlying securities (such as shares) without actually owning them outright.

cost base   Under the capital gains tax provisions, the price you pay for CGT assets such as shares. It also includes your acquisition and disposal costs (for instance, brokerage fees and GST).

crystallise   This means disposing of shares in order to create or realise a capital gain or capital loss for taxation purposes.

derived   Income you receive or earn that's liable to tax.

directors   Appointed by shareholders to manage and run the day-to-day operations of the company.

discount capital gain   A capital gain on disposal of CGT assets such as shares that were owned for at least 12 months. Only half the capital gain you make on disposal is liable to tax. The other half is exempt.

discretionary trust   A trust where the trustee has discretion as to how the trust net income should be distributed to the beneficiaries.

dividend   A distribution of profit you receive from a company because you are a part owner. The amount you receive depends on the number of shares you own.

dividend franking credit   A tax offset you receive from a dividend that is franked.

dividend reinvestment plan   An agreement with the company that gives you the right to receive additional shares (normally at a discount and no brokerage is payable) in lieu of receiving a cash dividend payment.

e-tax A free electronic lodgement service provided by the Tax Office to allow you to lodge your tax return online.

European-style This means the holder of an option or warrant has the right to buy or sell the underlying shares on the expiry date.

family discretionary trust A trust whose membership is ordinarily made up of family beneficiaries. The trustee has discretion to distribute trust net income to certain family beneficiaries.

final dividend A dividend paid at the end of the financial year.

financial year Australia's financial year commences on 1 July and ends on 30 June.

foreign tax credit Foreign tax paid on income derived from overseas sources that can be offset against Australian tax payable on taxable income derived from worldwide sources.

franked dividend A dividend that gives you the right to receive a franking tax offset or credit. The offset is applied against the tax payable.

fundamental analysis Analysing published financial reports to check the financial stability of a company's business activities, and examining current economic conditions to assess whether a company's share price is likely to rise or fall.

goods and services tax (GST) A 10 per cent tax on goods and services, payable on your purchases and sales. No GST is payable on share transactions, but you're liable to pay GST on your brokerage fees.

grossed-up (grossing-up) This means including both the dividend and franking credit you receive as part of your taxable income. You will be taxed on the total amount and the franking credit is applied against the tax payable.

holder identification number (HIN) An identification number you receive under the CHESS system that is used when you buy or sell shares through a particular stockbroker.

holding statement A statement you receive from a company confirming the number of shares you own.

income tax A federal tax that you pay on taxable income you derive.

income tax return A form you lodge with the Australian Taxation Office each year disclosing your taxable income.

incurred A point in time when you can legally claim a tax deduction. This normally arises when you're *definitely committed* and have a *legal obligation to make a payment* for certain goods and services you receive.

instalment activity statement A statement under the pay-as-you-go system that you prepare at the end of each reporting period disclosing certain income that is liable to tax.

interest The amount of money you pay over and above repaying the principal amount when you borrow money to buy shares.

interim dividend A dividend that is normally paid mid-year.

interpretative decision An Australian Taxation Office ruling relating to a specific issue.

investment strategy A document that sets out how you intend to invest your benefits in a self managed superannuation fund. It must be in writing and must consider investment risks, the likely return on your investments, and whether you have sufficient cash on hand to discharge liabilities when they fall due.

joint ownership Owning investments jointly (for instance, as husband and wife).

line of credit loan A loan where you can access finance up to an approved predetermined limit.

listed company A company listed on the Australian Securities Exchange (ASX). Shares and securities of listed companies can be traded on the ASX.

low income tax offset A general tax offset you can claim if your taxable income is below a certain threshold (currently $30 000, per 2010–11 tax rates). The tax offset is reduced by four cents for every dollar you earn above this threshold.

managed funds Mutual or pooled investment funds managed by Australia's leading financial institutions (such as banks and insurance companies) that give investors the opportunity to invest in a wide range of domestic and foreign investment portfolios.

marginal rate of tax   The rate of tax payable on the last taxable income dollar you earn. The rate can vary from 0 per cent to 45 per cent (see the Tax Office website for the latest published rates).

margin loans   A financial arrangement where you'll use a combination of your own capital and borrowings to fund a share portfolio. If the value of your shares falls you'll be liable to make good the shortfall (referred to as a margin call).

market price   The current value of an asset that you can buy or sell on the open market.

Medicare levy   A medical levy based on a percentage of your taxable income (currently 1.5 per cent).

negative gearing   A term associated with borrowing money to buy wealth-creation assets such as shares. You will be negative gearing when your expenses (particularly interest payments) exceed the income you derive. Your expenses are then offset against other income earned, to reduce the tax you would otherwise pay.

net income   The amount of income that's left over when you deduct your allowable deductions from your assessable income.

net loss   A loss that arises when your allowable deductions exceed your assessable income.

non-capital costs   Non-deductible expenditure such as interest that can be included in the cost base of shares acquired after 20 August 1991 that pay no dividends.

non-discount capital gain   A capital gain on disposal of CGT assets that you had owned for less than 12 months. The entire capital gain is liable to tax.

non-renounceable rights issue   This means shareholders only can exercise their right to buy additional shares issued by the company. If they do not exercise their right the offer will lapse.

non-resident of Australia   A person who does not normally reside in Australia and has no intention of living here. Non-residents are liable to pay tax only on income sourced in Australia.

notice of assessment   The statement you receive from the Tax Office after you lodge your tax return summarising the details in your tax return.

objection   A formal challenge against a Tax Office assessment or decision.

offer   The price at which you are prepared to sell your shares in a company.

ordinary share   A class of share that gives shareholders the right to vote and receive a dividend and any capital distributions. Shareholders who hold these shares are paid last if a company is wound up.

partnership   Under Australian tax law persons in receipt of income jointly (for instance, husband and wife) are considered to be in partnership.

pay-as–you-go (PAYG) withholding tax Employers have a statutory obligation to withhold a certain amount of tax from an employee's pay and remit the amount to the Tax Office.

personal loans These are normally unsecured loans that you can take out for a specific purpose (for instance, to buy shares).

positive gearing A term associated with borrowing money to buy wealth-creation assets such as shares. You are positive gearing when your investment income (cash inflows) exceeds your investment expenses (cash outflows).

premium A price you pay to purchase an option or warrant.

presently entitled The right of a beneficiary of a trust to demand an immediate distribution of the trust's net income.

preservation age The age you must reach before you can access your superannuation fund benefits. Depending on when you're born this can vary from 55 to 60 years of age.

preserved benefits Superannuation fund benefits that you can access when you reach your preservation age and retire.

private ruling Written advice you receive from the Tax Office about how it would interpret the tax laws in respect of a specific issue you raise.

prospectus   A legal document that must be issued by companies wanting to raise finance. It sets out the terms and conditions of the loan and other matters required by law.

put option   A form of insurance that gives the holder the right, but not the obligation, to sell the underlying shares at an agreed price on or before the expiry date. A put option is worth buying in a falling market.

put warrant   Gives the holder the right, but not the obligation, to sell the underlying shares to the issuer (usually a financial institution) at an agreed price on or before the expiry date.

reduced cost base   The cost base of a CGT asset minus certain expenditure that had been allowed as a tax deduction. It's used to calculate a capital loss.

renounceable rights issue   This means shareholders can exercise their right to buy additional shares issued by the company or sell their rights on the Australian Securities Exchange.

resident of Australia   A person who normally resides in Australia (it can also include a company or trust). Residents are taxed on their worldwide income.

return of capital   Arises when a company returns capital to shareholders. A capital return does not constitute a dividend, and you'll need to reduce the cost base and reduced cost base of your shareholdings. If the return of capital is more than the cost base, the difference is treated as a capital gain.

rights issue The right to buy additional shares direct from the company at a specified price (usually below market price) on a specified future date. A rights issue is usually linked to the number of shares you hold. The rights may be sold on the Australian Securities Exchange.

S&P/ASX 200 index This is a Standard & Poor's index that comprises the top 200 companies listed on the Australian Securities Exchange and represents 90 per cent of total market capitalisation.

security reference number (SRN) An identification number issued by a company at the time you buy its shares.

self-assessment The Australian tax system works on a self-assessment basis. This means the onus is on you to declare to the Tax Office the correct amount of income you derive each year and claim the correct amount of tax deductions and tax offsets.

self managed superannuation fund A superannuation fund that you manage yourself.

sell contract note The invoice you receive from a stockbroker at the time you sell your shares. It will summarise the details of the transaction and can be used to calculate a capital gain or capital loss for taxation purposes.

shareholder A person who owns shares in a company.

shareholder dividend statement A statement you receive from a company at the time of the payment of a dividend. It will summarise the details of the payment and should be retained for taxation purposes.

share investor   A person who invests in the sharemarket with the predominant purpose of deriving dividends and long-term capital growth.

shares   Associated with the ownership of a company. Shares entitle you to receive a dividend and any return of capital and vote at the annual general meeting.

share split   Increasing the number of issued shares in direct proportion to the number of shares shareholders currently hold in an attempt to make the share price more affordable. Under the CGT provisions you'll need to reduce the cost base of each share you own.

share trader   A person who is carrying on a business trading in shares and/or derivatives with the predominant purpose of making a profit; also known as a day trader.

share trust   Mutual fund that invests in a wide range of Australian and overseas companies.

stockbroker   A person authorised to buy and sell shares on the Australian Securities Exchange. They charge a brokerage fee for their services.

stop loss   A strategy you use to reduce your exposure to potential losses; for instance, you will sell your shares if they fall to a predetermined price.

superannuation fund   A fund set up to finance retirement strategies. Benefits normally cannot be accessed until you reach your preservation age and you retire from the workforce. A superannuation fund can pay you a pension.

taxable Australian property Assets owned by non-residents of Australia that are located in Australia and liable to capital gains tax when they are disposed of. Ordinarily shares listed on the Australian Securities Exchange that are owned by non-residents are not liable to CGT.

taxable income The amount of income that's liable to tax. Taxable income equals assessable income less allowable deductions.

tax agent A person who is authorised to give you advice in respect of managing your tax affairs and can lodge a tax return on your behalf. The fee they charge for their services is ordinarily a tax deductible expense.

tax file number A number issued by the Australian Taxation Office to identify individuals and companies who lodge tax returns. You may need to quote this number to companies that pay unfranked dividends.

tax offset A tax credit or rebate that you can use to reduce the amount of tax payable on taxable income you derive.

tax refund Money you get back from the Tax Office if your total tax credits (tax previously paid plus tax offsets) exceed the amount of tax you are liable to pay.

tax ruling A public ruling issued by the Tax Office to explain and clarify how the Taxation Commissioner interprets tax legislation in respect of a specific issue.

technical analysis Relying predominantly on share charts to assess share price trends and patterns to check whether share prices are likely to rise or fall. Also used to assess the best time to enter and exit the market and whether a company is undervalued or overvalued.

trust A legal obligation binding a person (the trustee) who has control over investment assets (for instance, a share portfolio) for the benefit of beneficiaries.

trustee A person responsible for administering and managing the trust property over which he or she has control for the benefit of the beneficiaries.

under a legal disability Indicates that a beneficiary of a trust is not in a legal position to deal with a trust distribution, such as a minor, a bankrupt or an insane person.

underlying shares The shares that you will actually buy or sell.

unfranked dividend A dividend that does not entitle you to receive a franking credit.

unit holders Investors who own units in a managed fund.

variable-rate loan A loan where interest rates will vary in line with the prevailing market.

warrant An option issued that gives the holder the right, but not the obligation, to buy from the issuer or sell to the issuer the underlying shares at an agreed price on or before the expiry date.

wash sale Selling shares to predominantly make a capital loss and gain a tax benefit, then buying the shares back immediately.

withholding tax Tax that was withheld from a payment of income such as dividends that was paid to a non-resident of Australia.

Appendix A
Key historic dates: shares and taxation

1 July 1985

Company tax rate 46 per cent.

19 September 1985

Introduction of capital gains tax (CGT) provisions: capital gains on disposal of shares liable to tax; shares acquired before 20 September 1985 excluded from CGT provisions.

1 July 1986

Company tax rate increased from 46 per cent to 49 per cent.

1 April 1987

Formation of Australian Stock Exchange Limited (ASX).

Creation of National Guarantee Fund (investor compensation fund in respect of breaches of ASX rules as specified in the Corporations Act).

1 July 1987

Introduction of dividend imputation; shareholders can claim franking credits if dividends are franked.

Abolition of private company undistributed profits tax.

19 October 1987

World stock market crash of 1987.

Introduction of SEATS (Stock Exchange Automated Trading System).

1 July 1988

Company tax rate decreased from 49 per cent to 39 per cent.

July 1989

Introduction of FAST (Flexible Accelerated Security Transfer).

Companies permitted to buy back their own shares.

Companies can carry forward tax losses for an indefinite period; private companies must satisfy stringent tests to access prior year losses.

Corporations Act 1989 enacted.

Merger of Australian options market and financial futures market.

1 January 1991

Australian Securities Commission established to administer Australian Corporations Law (later renamed Australian Securities & Investments Commission (ASIC) from 1 July 1998).

New national scheme for corporate regulation commences.

10 January 1991

Beginning of trading in warrants on ASX.

21 August 1991

'Non-capital costs' such as interest on borrowings to buy shares that pay no dividends can form part of cost base of shares.

11 November 1991

New tax rules for deemed disposal and reacquisition of worthless shares held in companies in liquidation (liquidator declarations) introduced.

March 1992

T+5 (trade day plus five business days) settlement introduced.

1 July 1993

Company tax rate decreased from 39 per cent 33 per cent.

12 January 1994

New taxation rules in respect of material shifts in value of shares held by a person who 'controls' a company introduced.

1 September 1994

Introduction of CHESS (Clearing House Electronic Subregister System).

1 July 1995

Company tax rate increased from 33 per cent to 36 per cent.

December 1995

New simplified rules for share buybacks introduced.

13 May 1997

Forty-five-days holding rule introduced: shareholders must own shares for at least 45 days (90 days for preference shares) to qualify for franking credit tax offset. Small shareholder exemption provisions apply.

27 October 1997

World stock market crash of 1997.

4 December 1997

Private company payments, loans (and debts forgiven) to shareholders treated as unfranked dividends. Must enter into commercial loan agreement.

1 July 1998

New rules for taxing bonus shares introduced.

Abolition of par value of shares (share premium accounts).

13 October 1998

Australian Stock Exchange listed on the ASX.

1 January 1999

Phasing-out of issuing paper share certificates to shareholders. ASX listed companies to issue holding statements to record future share ownership.

1 February 1999

T+3 (trade day plus three business days) settlement deadline introduced.

21 September 1999

Changes to the way a capital gain is calculated introduced.

10 December 1999

Introduction of scrip-for-scrip capital gains tax rollover relief.

3 April 2000

Standard & Poor's index services takes over business index development from ASX.

7 April 2000

Stock market crash of 2000 (collapse of 'dotcom' companies).

1 July 2000

Introduction of a 10 per cent goods and services tax (GST): share transactions not liable to GST, but GST is payable on brokerage fees.

Company tax rate decreased from 36 per cent to 34 per cent.

Excess dividend franking credits refunded to resident shareholders.

Removal of inter-corporate dividend rebate in respect of unfranked dividends (unless dividend paid within wholly owned group).

1 July 2001

Company tax rate decreased from 34 per cent to 30 per cent.

Stamp duty payable on share transactions abolished.

New tax rules in respect of debt and equity in a company introduced.

15 July 2001

Corporations Act 2001 enacted.

11 September 2001

Fall in world stock markets following terrorist attacks on New York and Washington. The All Ordinaries index falls 9.9 per cent (from 3183.3 to 2867.4) over a two-week period.

March 2002

Contracts for difference introduced in Australia.

14 May 2002

New rules for taxing convertible notes into shares introduced.

1 July 2002

Simplified Imputation System (SIS) relating to franking accounts introduced.

New taxation rules allowing co-operative companies to frank dividends introduced.

New taxation rules relating to demergers introduced.

Introduction of tax consolidation regime — taxing wholly owned corporate groups as single entities (optional but irrevocable).

General value-shifting regime introduced — valuation of shares.

22 November 2002

ASX announces establishment of new body called Australian Clearing House (a clearing and settlement facility in respect of products traded on ASX).

12 December 2002

New rules for taxing trustee of trust estate and shareholders of private company introduced.

1 April 2003

New trans-Tasman dividend imputation rules introduced.

16 April 2003

Amended legislation introduced to limit claim for interest payable in respect of limited recourse equity loans, amount disallowed being a 'capital protection fee'. Legislation reverses full federal court decision in *FCT v Firth* to allow interest deduction in full.

22 March 2005

New rules for taxing shares that become worthless for CGT purposes introduced.

27 May 2005

New capital gains tax rules relating to taxation of options introduced.

25 July 2006

Merger of Australian Stock Exchange and Sydney Futures Exchange: now known as the Australian Securities Exchange (ASX) (as from 5 December 2006).

12 December 2006

New CGT rules for taxing non-residents introduced: Australian listed shares held by non-residents ordinarily excluded from CGT provisions.

31 January 2007

High Court landmark decision (*Sons of Gwalia v Margaretic*): inadequate market disclosure — under certain circumstances shareholders can recover funds from insolvent company (rank equal with unsecured creditors).

22 February 2007

High Court decision (*FCT v McNeil*): value of 'sell back rights' under St George Bank share buyback arrangement assessable income. (Tax Act subsequently amended to restore principal to tax rights issued by companies on capital account — CGT provisions.)

1 July 2007

Shares in listed public companies donated to deductible gift recipient eligible for a tax deduction.

New rules relating to deductibility of interest under a capital-protected borrowing arrangement for shares introduced.

New tax rules in respect of demutualisation of private health insurers introduced.

24 September 2007

Self managed superannuation funds can invest in instalment warrants (provided certain rules are met).

1 November 2007

S&P/ASX All Ordinaries index peaks at 6853.6 points.

22 September 2008

Australian Securities & Investments Commission (ASIC) imposes temporary ban on covered short-term selling of financial securities (ban lifted on 25 May 2009).

6 March 2009

S&P/ASX All Ordinaries index plunges 54.6 per cent from a high 6853.6 points on 1 November 2007 to a low of 3111.7 points on 6 March 2009 (global financial crisis).

1 May 2009

Stockbrokers must inform shareholders of rights and obligations in respect of trading partly paid securities (broker must receive signed agreement from shareholder).

1 July 2009

New rules for taxing employee share schemes introduced.

1 January 2010

New rules regulating margin lending arrangements commences (administered by Australian Securities & Investments Commission).

6 January 2010

New tax rules to defer capital gains tax relating to scrip-for-scrip rollover in respect of takeovers and mergers approved under the *Corporations Act 2001* introduced.

2 May 2010

Release of the Henry review of the Australian tax system.

Appendix B

Taxing non-residents of Australia

Under Australian tax law non-residents of Australia are liable to pay tax only on assessable income that has an Australian source. This will only become an issue if you're a non-resident currently residing in Australia or you have investments located in Australia. In order to avoid double taxation Australia has entered into international double tax agreements with a number of foreign countries. If you want to know whether Australia has a double tax agreement with a foreign country you can read Tax Office publication *Countries that have a tax treaty with Australia*.

At a glance: taxing non-residents

This is how a non-resident is taxed in Australia:

- Non-residents are liable to pay tax on a progressive basis at non-resident rates on income that has an Australian source; non-residents are not entitled to a $6000 tax-free threshold.

- Non-residents are not liable to pay a Medicare levy.

- Non-residents cannot claim domestic tax offsets such as franking credits.

- Unfranked dividends are only liable to withholding tax; the rate of tax payable depends on whether Australia has a double tax treaty with the applicable foreign country.

- No withholding tax payable to the extent the dividend is franked.

- Non-residents are only liable to pay capital gains tax on taxable Australian property. Shares listed on the ASX are ordinarily excluded from these provisions.

 Tax trap

In ATO interpretative decision ID 2004/904 it was held that profits derived by a non-resident taxpayer from carrying on a business as a trader in shares and options in Australian entities are assessable in Australia as the source of the profit is in Australia.

Dividends

A non-resident of Australia who derives unfranked dividends from an Australian resident company is only liable to pay withholding tax. The amount of tax the company will withhold depends on whether Australia had entered into a double tax agreement with the country where the non-resident resides. Ordinarily the rate is 15 per cent if a double tax agreement exists with a foreign country and 30 per cent if there is no double tax agreement. If a non-resident receives a franked dividend the rate of tax withheld is reduced to the extent the dividend is franked. This means if a non-resident receives a fully franked dividend no withholding tax is withheld from the dividend payment. Non-residents cannot claim a refund of excess franking credits as is the case if you are a resident of Australia.

 Tax tip

Dividends derived by a non-resident of Australia which are liable to withholding tax only are excluded from assessable income. This means a non-resident is not required to lodge an Australian tax return in respect of the dividends derived. If a non-resident is required to lodge an Australian tax return disclosing other Australian-sourced income, the dividends will be excluded from assessable income.

Australia has entered into double tax agreements with the following countries, with a withholding tax rate of 15 per cent:

- Canada
- China
- India
- Japan
- Korea
- Indonesia
- Malaysia
- New Zealand
- Singapore
- South Africa
- United Kingdom
- United States.

Capital gains tax (CGT)

As a general rule non-resident share investors who buy and sell shares listed on the ASX are not liable to pay capital gains tax on disposal of their shares. This is because non-residents are liable to pay CGT only on 'taxable Australian property', and shares listed on the ASX are ordinarily excluded from these provisions. For more details you can read Tax Office publication *Capital gains in Australia*.

Tax tip

Whether you're a non-resident of Australia is a question of fact. The Australian Taxation Office has issued two tax rulings that deal with this matter. They are taxation rulings IT 2650: *Income tax: residency—permanent place of abode outside Australia* and TR 98/17: *Income tax: residency status of individuals entering Australia*. You can get a copy from the ATO or you can visit its website <www.ato.gov.au>.

Useful references

Australian Taxation Office publications

- *Australian income of foreign residents—overview*

- *CGT on foreign residents, temporary residents and changing residency*

- Fact sheet: 'Taxation of trust net income—non resident beneficiaries—general overview of the changes'

- *Income from dividends—non-residents*

- *Investing in Australia—overview*

- *New withholding arrangements for managed fund distributions to foreign residents*

- *Non-residents—lodging an Australian income tax return*

- *PAYG withholding for interest, dividends, and royalties paid to non-residents* (NAT 12564)

- *Reporting non-resident withholding from interest and dividend payments*

Australian Taxation Office interpretative decisions

- ID 2001/186: *Income tax: withholding tax—New Zealand resident in receipt of dividends from Australian resident company*

- ID 2002/94: *Income tax: trustee of a trust with a non-resident beneficiary (unfranked dividends)*

- ID 2003/854: *Income tax: assessability of Australian sourced dividend income received by a UK resident*

- ID 2004/141: *Income tax: assessability of dividends received by a dual resident of Australia and the United States*

- ID 2009/78: *ivncome tax: non-assessable and non-exempt income—dividends: non-share dividends and interest of a superannuation fund for foreign resident*

Index